MICHAL SPIEGELMAN

BECOMING SOULFUL

ISBN 9798990542402 (paperback)

ISBN 9798990542419 (epub)

Published 2024

Cover design by Kam Bains

Illustrations by Shawn Muller

Visit the author's website at beaconsofchange.com

This book is dedicated to the quiet heroes: therapists, coaches, and healers who pour their hearts into transforming lives for the better, and to the countless generous spirits and natural givers who, without title or acclaim, light up the path of transformation for others with their presence.

PRAISE

"Michal Spiegelman's deep dive into the transformative powers of self-awareness and authenticity offers an actionable and profound path for those ready to realize their full potential and bring forth the change they wish to see in their lives and practices."

Bruce D Schneider
Founder, The Institute for Professional Excellence in Coaching, and author of *Energy Leadership and Uncovering the Life of Your Dreams*

"Michal Spiegelman's *Becoming Soulful* echoes the Hoffman Institute's mission of fostering personal freedom and holistic transformation. The book's framework of six keys offers profound paths toward liberation and authenticity, guiding individuals toward a life of authenticity, emotional intelligence, and conscious choice. Michal's wisdom mirrors the transformative experiences that the Institute champions. Celebrating Michal's roots in our teachings, this work is a beacon that extends the reach of our shared vision into the world."

Liza Ingrasci
President and CEO, Hoffman Institute Foundation

"*Becoming Soulful* is a rare find that integrates tested methods, practical exercises, and deep spiritual insights into a comprehensive framework. Spiegelman offers us a hopeful blueprint and much-needed navigational clarity on how to build a better world centered on a forgotten and underused resource: our self-knowledge and soul wisdom. The nuggets she gathers and highlights along the inner journey are brilliant, transformational, and enriching, and both beginner and seasoned practitioners will find many valuable treasures to add to their toolbox."

Loraine Van Tuyl, PhD
Author of *Soul Authority: Liberatory Tools to Heal from Oppressive Patterns and Restore Trust in Your Heart Compass*

"In *Becoming Soulful*, Michal invites us to engage more deeply with the full range of our human experience as spiritual beings. With stories and exercises that illustrate each aspect of soulfulness, Michal makes the process of exploration, growth, and the development of competency in the spiritual realm of healing accessible and engaging for therapists, coaches, and healers from a variety of backgrounds and perspectives. As a therapist who values all aspects of my clients' identities, *Becoming Soulful* has emerged as an extremely valuable part of my therapeutic library. Michal brings awareness to the hidden power of soulfulness within us all and empowers us with the tools needed to engage this core aspect of self within us and our clients. I am so grateful for this resource full of practices and tangible ways to expand my therapeutic work into this essential realm."

Cindy Wander, MA, MS, LPC, LMFT

"A must-read for practitioners dedicated to deep, impactful work, *Becoming Soulful* delivers wisdom and insights coupled with practical exercises and guided visualizations to provide a solid framework that facilitates healing and growth and fosters a deeper understanding of the human soul."

Liz Phillips Fisch, MEd, PCC
Retired Senior Vice President, The Institute for Professional
Excellence in Coaching

"Michal Spiegelman's *Becoming Soulful* beautifully weaves practical wisdom with deep reflection, the spiritual with the somatic, the personal with the professional, and guidance with grace. She offers a brilliant constellation of insight, self-discovery, and hope for all who read it—especially for those of us who long to invite transformation into the lives of those with and for whom we work."

Ronna Detrick
Speaker/Coach and Author of *Rewriting Eve: Rescuing Women's Stories From the Bible and Reclaiming Them as Our Own*

"Michal Spiegelman's work redefines professional engagement in therapy, coaching, and the healing arts. Exploring each key offers a transformative path to those seeking to empower their service approach. *Becoming Soulful* is essential for those on the path to true personal and professional fulfillment. As someone fortunate enough to know and work with Michal, this book resonates strongly with her authenticity and deep concern for the welfare of professionals."

Laura Silverman, LCSW
Owner, Sweetgrass Integrative Counseling and Therapy and Sweetgrass Wellness

CONTENTS

INTRODUCTION

I had tears of joy in my eyes as I accepted my social work degree on a sunny summer day in 1987. I was overwhelmed with gratitude stepping up to the stage in my graduation gown and mortarboard, eager to solidify my born desire to help others. However, it didn't take long before I was challenged by the limitations of my education and abilities. My new job proved emotionally draining, and I found it less fulfilling than I had imagined. I felt something vital was absent from my therapeutic resources. Despite learning some of the latest theories and practices at the time, my approach to healing was narrow. I had little understanding of the body as an energy storehouse and lacked the skills to see the person as a whole.

Eventually, I followed my inner call, broadening my approach to include holistic methods: Reiki, meditation, color healing, and bodywork. This expansion allowed me to enhance the therapeutic journey by integrating the healing of mind, body, spirit, *and soul.*

It was years later when that same guiding voice within urged me to seek out new tools and delve deeper into my capabilities. Another defining moment unfolded at the conclusion of a weekend training with my life-coaching school, The Institute for Professional Excellence in Coaching (iPEC). We engaged in a lighthearted, playful exercise where we, the aspiring coaches, were tasked with responding to scenarios and demonstrating our coaching strategies. I found myself in the spotlight, rising to the challenge and eventually being celebrated as the victor of the coaching exercise. During the applause, a sense of sacredness enveloped me, reminding me of the humility and gratitude I experienced at my social work graduation. Filled with anticipation, I looked forward to creating an even greater impact in the world.

Every time I was unknowingly ready to take the next evolution of my work, my inner voice nudged me to step out of my comfort zone. As a medical intuitive, spiritual mentor, and founder of the Beacons of Change community, I had reached a high point of fulfillment. Using my training in a wide range of healing modalities, along with my intuitive nature, I support women in uncovering the root causes of their physical symptoms, stress, and trauma-related conditions. And then I help them heal.

Empowering women to live, love, and lead at full power fills me up. Yet once more, it was the whisper of my Soul that encouraged me on to encapsulate the trauma-informed healing method I had honed over three decades. With immense honor, I introduce this language, process, and framework through the pages of this book.

You may find echoes of your own journey in mine, or perhaps your story weaves a different path. Consider this book your personal invitation to discover and cultivate a therapeutic approach that is distinctly yours.

In a world that often overlooks the deep impact of your work, I want to take a moment to honor your incredible dedication, your commitment to healing, and the transformative power you bring to your clients. As a seasoned therapist, coach, or healing professional, you possess an extraordinary gift—the ability to guide others through profound self-discovery, growth, and transformation.

But even as you stand at the forefront of healing, your Soul may be hungry for ways to delve deeper, to unlock the doors that hold the keys to lasting change. Your passion for helping people and positively impacting their lives may have led you to crave even more depth and meaning in the therapeutic process.

You care deeply about your clients and don't want them to merely cope with their challenges. You strive to help them heal at a deeper level, uncovering the underlying causes of their behaviors, struggles, and symptoms. While you already use tools that go beyond surface-level insights, you yearn to embrace a wider variety of holistic methods. You value practices like mindfulness and self-regulation techniques, but you're also curious about alternative approaches that can support your clients during difficult moments in sessions.

You find yourself wondering just how deep you can go to truly get to the core of your clients' experiences. You're open to learning additional approaches that can help address the root issues in new ways.

You may notice that some clients experience unresolved physical symptoms alongside their emotional struggles, such as chronic pain, tension, digestive issues, and fatigue. You're eager to find practical ways to complement your existing work and address these symptoms more effectively. Deep down, you know that there are alternative tools and approaches to release stress and trauma stored in the body, but you may lack the time, resources, or knowledge to explore them.

At times, you may feel like something is missing—a mysterious element that could bring more depth to your work. This element, once vague, will unfold and become clarified as you navigate through the pages of this book.

In your quest for direction, you yearn for a toolbox filled with creative and effective techniques. You want to be armed with the means to guide clients toward genuine transformation, moving beyond intellectual understanding to heartfelt healing experiences. When clients carry the weight of trauma and struggle to connect with their pain, you seek to address the embedded stress and trauma within their bodies, forging a path toward sustainable healing.

Not only do you aspire to make a difference in your clients' lives, but you also long to enhance your own professional abilities. You understand that being more empowered, grounded, and centered as a therapist will profoundly affect your work. There may be moments when you question your solidity as a professional and desire support and guidance to navigate these challenges.

Drawing from extensive conversations with therapists, coaches, and healing professionals over the years, I have crafted a set of 15 questions to assist you in recognizing and understanding your unique needs and aspirations as a professional.

Consider each question below and reflect on your own experiences and aspirations:

1. What changes have you observed in the levels of emptiness, lack of meaning, anxiety, and depression among your clients?

2. In what ways do you sense a gap in your practice despite being a trained healing professional?

3. How deep do you believe you can go to uncover the underlying issues driving your clients' behaviors, struggles, or symptoms?

4. How open are you to learning additional holistic approaches to address the root causes of your clients' challenges?

5. How eager are you to facilitate deeper healing for your clients beyond helping them cope with their difficulties?

6. How curious are youÍ about alternative methods for supporting your clients through challenging moments, aside from mindfulness and self-regulation techniques?

7. What would be the impact on your practice if you integrated practices that address unresolved physical symptoms like chronic pain, tension, digestive issues, or fatigue, thereby offering more comprehensive care for your clients?

8. How strongly do you believe in the potential of alternative tools to release stress and trauma stored in the body?

9. How would your practice evolve if you had access to learning new tools directly, bypassing the need for extensive personal research and resource investment?

10. How would becoming more grounded and centered as a therapist enhance your professional abilities and the quality of care you provide to your clients?

11. How open are you to integrating spiritual yet non-religious elements in your practice while ensuring a safe and comfortable space for your client?

12. What level of excitement would you feel about introducing a new approach that complements talk therapy and fosters the integration of mind and body for your clients?

13. What doors would open for you professionally and personally if you were to rediscover the joy in your work that aligns with your deep passion for helping others?

14. How willing are you to embrace the role of a lasting healing presence in your clients' lives, transcending the role of a short-term crisis resource, to enhance client retention and deepen therapeutic relationships?

15. How important is it for you to cultivate a distinct identity that distinguishes you from your peers and allows you to stand out within your field?

As you engage with these questions, what clarity emerges for you? Do you feel a sense of pride as you reflect on how far you've come and a longing to uncover the missing pieces that can enhance your ability to bring depth to your work? A touch of frustration or discomfort may arise from grappling with these challenging inquiries. Maybe you yearn for more time and resources that could provide a greater sense of professional fulfillment.

I want you to know that you are not alone. Many professionals find themselves caught up in the demands of running their business, leaving little time to explore, research, or develop new methods to expand their work. It can be overwhelming to think about where to even begin if you do have the time.

We professionals hold the power to be catalysts for change in this world, and that transformation begins within ourselves. However, three crucial elements often hinder us from living happy, healthy lives and unleashing our full potential:

 ~ A lack of engagement with a form of spirituality that acknowledges a power greater than ourselves
 ~ A separation from our Soul
 ~ A disconnection from our body

It is essential that we fearlessly confront these challenges; incorporate soulful, spiritual, and somatic work into our personal and professional lives; and expand our impact and presence.

Thank you for joining me on this important mission to elevate consciousness in the world, one Soulful Healer at a time. Together, we aim to build a generation of professionals who create a deeper impact and establish a profound presence by integrating the Soulful Healer Method into their work.

Although this book primarily addresses therapists, coaches, and healing professionals, I warmly invite all women who are on their personal paths of self-discovery and transformation to delve into the 15 questions as well. Reflect on how each question might apply to your own journey toward a deeper relationship with yourself and others, toward living a more purposeful life, and toward having a meaningful impact on those around you. Whether you are seeking to enhance your personal well-being or to make a positive impact in your community, these questions can serve as a guide to deeper self-awareness and purposeful action.

What Is a Soulful Healer?

A Soulful Healer embodies a therapy, coaching, or healing arts professional who adopts a comprehensive approach, integrating spiritual, soulful, and somatic practices within their work, while upholding the values and principles laid out in the Soulful Healers Manifesto.

A Soulful Healer is not confined to those with official titles or professional credentials. This term equally applies to individuals, particularly women, who are on a profound journey of self-discovery. These women strive to deepen their relationships with themselves and others, live a purposeful life, and make a significant positive impact both in their own lives and on those around them. They embody the essence of soulful healing by integrating it into their daily living, proving that the path of a Soulful Healer is open to all who are called to it.

The Soulful Healers Manifesto

We stand together as a collective, knowing that healing together outshines healing alone.

We recognize the interconnectedness of the mind, body, spirit, and soul and champion an integrated approach to our sacred work.

We prioritize self-care.

We are humble yet confident in our gifts.

We navigate challenges with grace.

We listen to inner guidance, allowing our souls to speak.

We create safe spaces for healing.

We uncover root causes and lead with grounded wisdom.

As guides for transformation and self-discovery, we serve as conduits for healing, influencing the collective consciousness.

By embodying healing in our own lives, we facilitate healing in the lives of others.

Empowered to empower others, we create freedom inside and out.

Together, we infuse our lives with greater empowerment, spirituality, authenticity, insight, vitality, and embodiment.

In the symphony of healing, we are bound by a shared journey toward holistic well-being.

As one, we dance to the rhythm of our unique hearts and souls, expanding our impact and leaving a lasting mark on the world.

Our Soul has the potential to be a perfect guide.

She yearns for deeper meaning, expansion, and growth. She longs to guide us on the path of becoming Soulful Healers, empowering us to reach our full potential.

By becoming Soulful Healers, we contribute to alleviating the trauma, suffering, and pain that are so prevalent in today's world.

As you continue to explore the Soulful Healer Method through the pages of this book, you'll discover your unique ways to enhance your professional abilities, empowering you to guide clients toward genuine transformation. With a toolbox full of creative and effective approaches, you'll become the lasting presence your clients seek.

It is time to ask ourselves an important question: Why is it essential for us to embrace the path of becoming Soulful Healers?

Why We Need to Become Soulful Healers

The first therapist I worked with, while proficient in clinical therapeutic techniques from her training, didn't practice trauma-informed care or adopt a holistic approach. She was skilled at guiding me through past challenges and taking me back to my childhood experiences. However, she couldn't connect with my present state. There was a missing piece: the "here and now," the empathy and compassion I needed at the moment. I often left feeling diminished, craving to be seen, heard, and understood. The trauma we unpacked seemed to linger in me, leaving me burdened and increasingly sad. Eventually, I found the courage to acknowledge that she wasn't the right therapist for me.

If I had known then what I know now, I wouldn't have worked with her.

Even though my first therapist didn't address my trauma wisely, she was one of my greatest teachers. My experience with her made me want to learn more about the complexities of trauma and the importance of taking a mind–body approach to healing.

While each professional we work with is there to teach us something, our greatest teachers may be the ones who teach us what may be missing from the therapeutic process to make it effective and impactful.

The world is abundant with compassionate individuals, like me and you, who have dedicated our lives to the critical mission of healing and improving the world. Within the depths of our hearts, we are driven by a profound sense of pride and passion for our work, fueling a deep longing to become the guiding beacons we were meant to be on a larger scale.

We—therapists, coaches, and healing professionals—want to stand out from the crowd by creating a distinct identity that sets us apart from others in our field.

We desire to deepen our work and provide more depth and meaning in the therapeutic process.

We want to stand out and attract clients who resonate with our style and philosophy.

We are committed to learning. We know that good professionals are constantly working on themselves and continuing to grow.

How can we effectively support others if we struggle to stay afloat? We must acknowledge the importance of safeguarding our emotional and mental health while helping others heal.

Given the massive rise in awareness about trauma, we need to be responsible for using trauma-informed approaches, so we don't traumatize or retraumatize ourselves and others. As Soulful Healers, we must provide tangible methods for our clients to release the trauma stored in their bodies. It is crucial that we acknowledge and accept our limitations, recognizing that talk therapy alone may not be sufficient to guide our clients toward a profound emotional release from the pain and trauma they carry.

To truly facilitate a meaningful healing journey, we must continue to go beyond addressing surface-level symptoms and delve into the root causes of suffering. This involves understanding and honoring the interconnectedness of the mind, body, spirit, *and soul.* By embracing a holistic approach, we become more attuned to the soulful dimensions of our existence, integrating spiritual practices into our work and fostering a deeper connection with our own bodies. This expanded approach enhances our ability to maintain a soulful connection with our inner guidance system, making us feel more guided, directed, and equipped to help our clients navigate their transformation journeys.

In this challenging time of awakening, the world is experiencing many events and circumstances that have profoundly impacted individuals and societies. The collective energy on the planet is heavy as more and more people deal with feelings of depression, anxiety, and fatigue. The weight of suffering is affecting the immense challenges and transformations unfolding globally.

The process of awakening is calling professionals to step up and elevate their practice, to continuously evolve and expand their skills to effectively address the challenges and needs of individuals. Some of the tools and coping mechanisms that worked in the past may no longer be enough to navigate the complexities of the current world.

> *To address the increasing needs of those facing depression, anxiety, and fatigue, we must adopt a fresh perspective and view the world through a new lens. This lens will guide us to navigate the world's difficult complexities while equipping individuals with tools and support to reclaim their well-being. It enables us to not only seek external guidance but also turn inward and allow our Inner Wisdom to guide us, and to empower our clients to awaken to the wisdom of their souls as well.*

Now, once we understand the "what" and "why" of becoming a Soulful Healer, it is time to ask one more question.

How Do We Become Soulful Healers?

Becoming a Soulful Healer is a transformative journey that encompasses six essential qualities. These qualities serve as keys to unlock the door toward becoming the best version of ourselves, both personally and professionally. Each key will be presented in its own chapter in this book.

Through the process of *becoming soulful*, we discover our unique way to shine and make a positive impact in the world.

The six keys serve as catalysts for personal and professional growth. They unlock the doors, enabling us to bring more *empowerment, spirituality, authenticity, insight, vitality,* and *embodiment* into our professional lives.

Empowerment aligns us with our personal and professional qualities, inner strengths, and values. It instills within us a sense of confidence and solidity, enabling us to create positive change in the world.

Spirituality, when cultivated, deepens our connection with a power greater than us. This sacred bond broadens our consciousness and opens us to embrace infinite possibilities that go beyond our physical lives, fostering expansive personal growth.

Authenticity enables us to connect with the pure essence of our being, tapping into the truest version of ourselves and receiving inner guidance. Learning to seek guidance from within rather than relying solely on external sources enhances our professional abilities and makes us more adept at our craft.

Insight can come from various sources and moments in life, such as introspection, reflection, and self-awareness. However, we often underestimate the power of two potent sources of wisdom: Inner Wisdom and Collective Wisdom. Embracing and being receptive to insights from these sources can broaden our professional horizons and enhance our ability to provide exceptional care.

Vitality plays a crucial role when working with individuals who have experienced trauma and suffering. It is essential to have practical strategies in place to recharge our internal batteries and manage our energetic well-being so we can better support those in need and continue to provide compassionate care.

Embodiment deepens our connection with the fundamental wisdom of the body, fostering a harmonious alignment among mind, body, spirit, and soul. This alignment not only amplifies our healing capabilities but also enhances our ability to facilitate a more profound, transformative journey for those we serve.

This is your journey, our journey, toward becoming the Soulful Healers the world needs.

Together, we will navigate the path of learning, transformation, and personal mastery, creating a profound impact not only in the lives of our clients but also within ourselves.

> " As Soulful Healers, embracing these key elements unlocks the tremendous power within us, inspiring others to do the same. Together, we create a ripple effect of transformation and healing that extends far beyond our individual journeys.
>
> By doing so, we contribute to alleviating the trauma, suffering, and pain that are dominant in today's world. We have a world to change, and the change starts with us. "

Before We Begin

Before diving into the book, please visit my website to access and download complementary resources.

Scan the QR code below to easily find exercises, tracking forms, and maps that complement each chapter. These materials are optimized for printing, allowing you to engage with them more effectively.

Every chapter in this book is complemented by a guided visualization, carefully crafted to assist you in guiding your clients through transformative imagery. For your personal practice, audio versions of these visualizations are available for download, providing a convenient and immersive experience to accompany you through each journey.

https://beaconout.com/bsr

Chapter 1

KEY # 1—EMPOWERMENT
Reconnecting with Personal and Professional Power

Before You Begin, Download These Resources:

"Navigate the Sea of Possibilities" guided visualization audio and the "Soulful Healers Island of Possibilities" form in color.

https://beaconout.com/bsr

In my early 20s, I earned my degree in social work. Initially, I felt a rush of enthusiasm and pride from serving those in need. However, within a few short years these positive emotions were replaced by frustration, burnout, and physical and emotional exhaustion. Despite the skills I acquired in school, I could not handle the helplessness and disorientation of attempting to support people facing complex challenges.

As a young, inexperienced, and insecure social worker, I lacked an understanding of my inner resources and struggled to connect with them. Instead, I hunted for external solutions. Working within a bureaucratic government system, where there was a lack of professional support, only compounded my feelings of disempowerment and confusion.

Reflecting on this period of my life, I now understand that I had compromised my values. The value I placed on "service" was so high that it overshadowed my own needs and neglected other values important to me, such as self-care, balance, and joy. I was so focused on helping others that I disregarded the cost to my own health and happiness. This twisted perspective was partly due to my upbringing in a household that prioritized service to others over self-care. In hindsight, I see how this imbalance took a toll on me both physically and emotionally.

Our professional growth requires honoring our Soul's yearning to experience and enjoy life fully. It is about embracing joy, curiosity, and fulfillment as much as alleviating pain or suffering. This involves recognizing that we can only truly help others when we are also taking care of ourselves. It means understanding that self-care is not selfish, but essential, and that experiencing joy is not a luxury but a vital part of our journey. It is okay to highly value service or helping others, but we must balance giving and receiving, ensuring we equally prioritize self-care alongside caring for others.

Our values and attributes are foundational aspects that help us build a solid core. This core allows us to confidently show up in our personal and professional lives, sharing our light with the world.

The North Star of Life: Aligning Personal, Professional, and Collective Values

> *Consider life as sailing on a vast ocean where you are the ship's captain. Your task is to steer your vessel, keeping a keen eye on the horizon and weather conditions. In this grand voyage, your values serve as your North Star, guiding you through the journey. They are steering you toward a life of meaning and purpose and helping you stay true to yourself.*

Values are the deep-rooted principles that guide our decisions, actions, and behaviors. They remind us of what genuinely matters to us, driving our life's course, both personally and professionally, even when the way forward might seem unclear.

Personal Values: Our personal values shape how we show up in our day-to-day lives. They are sacred and close to our hearts.

Recognizing our personal values helps us understand what truly motivates us, what we consider essential, and what we aspire to achieve.

Professional Values: Our professional values define what's important to us as we step into our professional roles.

Identifying our professional values aids in aligning our professional choices with our personal beliefs, leading to increased satisfaction and success at work.

Collective Values: Collective values, particularly those critical to Soulful Healers, foster a shared environment of interconnectedness.

In my years of observing both the triumphs and challenges faced by those in the healing profession, I've crafted a list of shared values aimed at creating a sense of unity. This framework is meant to guide us to a common ground, fostering a spirit of interconnectedness essential for Soulful Healers. For professionals who find themselves not quite in step with these values, I recommend a period of introspection. This is an invitation to realign with these universal principles that I believe are fundamental to making a heartfelt and genuine contribution to the world.

Collective values enhance our healing abilities and contribute to a more harmonious, understanding, and connected world.

Defining our values creates an inner framework in which we can operate with authenticity and integrity. This framework guides our actions, decisions, and interactions, enabling us to positively impact ourselves and those around us.

When was the last time you made a list of what truly matters to you personally and professionally?

The discussions I have with people training to become Soulful Healers are always profoundly inspiring, especially when we explore the topic of values. Encouraging them to reflect on the distinctions between their personal and professional values often leads to thought-provoking questions. For example, is it necessary for personal and professional values to align? Are there any personal values that conflict with your professional ones? These conversations often guide them toward a better alignment with what truly matters to them, resulting in an increased sense of purpose and fulfillment in their personal and professional lives.

As we navigate our way to becoming Soulful Healers, we must understand and align our personal, professional, and collective values. You will have an opportunity to identify your unique personal and professional values later in this chapter, but first, let's explore a set of collective values that unite us as Soulful Healers.

This list of collective values for Soulful Healers has been carefully developed through extensive testing and numerous heartfelt conversations.

These values are not just words on a page but the guiding principles that define our community and shape our sacred roles.

Soulful Healers: Our Collective Values

1. *Authenticity:* Embracing and expressing our true selves, being genuine in our thoughts, actions, and interactions

2. *Community:* Building a supportive and inclusive community that fosters connection, collaboration, mutual purpose, and support

3. *Continuous Development:* Embracing ongoing curiosity, learning, and growth to enhance skills, knowledge, and wisdom

4. *Empowerment:* Empowering ourselves and others to reach their full potential

5. *Humanity:* Demonstrating love, care, and respect for all individuals, including ourselves

6. *Innovation:* Encouraging proactive, creative, and innovative thinking to explore new approaches, tools, and solutions

7. *Integrity:* Upholding unwavering ethical standards with honesty, transparency, and accountability in professional interactions

8. *Joy:* Cultivating an atmosphere of joy and positivity, celebrating life's moments, and fostering happiness in ourselves and those around us

9. *Leadership:* Leading by example with empathy and inspiration, accepting responsibly for nurturing personal growth, all while championing collaborative progress and individual empowerment

10. *Soulfulness:* Infusing our work with deep awareness, embracing the interconnectedness of mind, body, spirit, and soul in the healing process, honoring the essence of our being

Soulful Snapshot: Our Values in Action

The transformative impact of embracing and living by our values came to light during a trip to Europe, where two Soulful Healers were traveling together. Upon their return, one of the participants reported how her friend, Sarah, truly personified the essence of a Soulful Healer. Sarah seized every chance to provide healing treatments to those around her, demonstrating the principles of the Soulful Healers' shared vocation in action.

Before the trip, Sarah, an energy healer trained in Reiki, Eden Energy Medicine, Theta Healing, and Access Bars, set a personal intention to live out her core values of boldness, authenticity, and belonging. She viewed the trip as a chance to push beyond her usual limits. She wanted to feel part of the group they traveled with. Throughout the journey, she confidently embraced these values, often sensing when someone needed her healing touch.

On one occasion, when a group member was stung by a bee near his eye, Sarah's timely intervention significantly alleviated his pain. Sarah is traditionally more reserved; her proactive approach marked a departure from her past self-restraint. By stepping forward and offering her healing services, she helped others and reinforced her sense of belonging. This feeling had puzzled her in the past when she retreated into the background, especially within groups. Aligning with her values became her turning point, and Sarah has been sharing her gifts with others with confidence and courage since then. She offers healing sessions in a few locations. She is bolder and more confident both in her personal life and professional practice.

Sarah's story is a powerful testament to the strength of living true to one's values. Her experiences highlight how living in alignment not only transforms an individual but also radiates outwards, touching the lives of others.

" *Let your compass of values—personal, professional, and collective—be your North Star illuminating your path, bringing meaning to your journey, and anchoring your role as a Soulful Healer in the world.* "

Understanding Attributes: The Building Blocks of Our Identity

Let's now turn our focus to another crucial aspect of our personal and professional identity—our attributes.

While values guide our decisions and actions, our attributes define who we are at our core, and create our personal power.

" *Attributes are the extraordinary qualities that make each of us unique. They highlight our individuality and inspire us to stand out and make our mark in exceptional ways.* "

Attributes are the traits and characteristics we possess, originating from our genetic makeup and environmental influences. They significantly shape our personality, influence our behavior, and, ultimately, determine how we interact with the world around us.

Just as a ship is built with unique features to tolerate the ocean's waves, we are gifted with a unique combination of attributes that equip us to navigate life's challenges. Identifying and understanding these attributes is just as important as recognizing our values. They form the building blocks of our identity, influencing our strengths, weaknesses, and potential for growth.

Attributes, like values, are dynamic, evolving with our experiences, learnings, and personal development. Some attributes may become more noticeable as we journey through life, while others may take a backseat. Some may feel natural, while others are cultivated over time.

Think back to your childhood. Were you creative? Playful? Did you experience life with a sense of joy and wonder? How have those attributes evolved as you've grown into adulthood? To what extent do you show traits from childhood in your personal and professional life as an adult?

Many professionals in our community who are proficient and highly knowledgeable in their fields have reported that recognizing and owning their inner gifts have strengthened their confidence in their work. This heightened self-belief is quite noticeable, allowing them to trust themselves more and help their clients improve.

Later in this chapter, you can select a list of attributes that reflect your core self. Consider which characteristics you feel more connected to now compared to the past and which ones you'd like to connect with more deeply in the future.

Another interesting aspect is whether others' perceptions of your attributes align with yours. If you asked other people to describe you, would they list the same characteristics, or is there a difference between how you view yourself and how others see you?

It's also worth reflecting on your professional persona. Are the attributes that define you personally the same as those you express professionally? This can offer insightful revelations about your personal and professional development.

Empowerment arises from combining personal values and attributes, which together build a strong sense of self. It's our Soul's purpose to live true to our values and fully embody our unique qualities. This alignment is what defines us and steers our journey through life.

> *Aligning with your values and embracing your attributes unlocks your personal power, which is the essence of self-directed life and the source of your inner strength.*

Why Empowerment Is the Heartbeat of Transformation

Let's look at why we start the journey to becoming a Soulful Healer connecting to attributes and values. Traditional therapeutic approaches often focus predominantly on past traumas and issues, which undeniably are crucial parts of the healing process. Those methods focus on desensitizing the traumatic event. Creating a safe space to re-expose the wounded person to their trauma can reduce outbursts and flashbacks.

However, as a therapist, coach, or healing professional, it's equally essential for you to help your clients recognize and connect with their inner strength and potential in the present. By doing so, you're assisting in healing their past and empowering them to live life to the fullest in the present.

> *Holistic healing is a dual journey, addressing both the past and the present. Each path is equally important in achieving complete wellness.*

I love the work of psychiatrist Bessel van der Kolk, the author of the #1 *New York Times* bestseller *The Body Keeps the Score: Brain, Mind, and Body in the Healing of Trauma*. He studied the treatment of post-traumatic stress in civilians (adults and children). In his book, van der Kolk suggests that talking about distressing feelings is not enough to resolve them. Healing can take place only when people start to notice, feel, and put into words the reality of their internal experience *in the moment*.

According to van der Kolk, healing is not a linear process that ends with resolving past traumas; instead, it's an ongoing practice of being present and engaged in life. He emphasizes that true healing involves creating experiences in the present that can foster the growth of new, positive associations and pathways in the brain.

This present-focused approach allows individuals to redefine their identity not by what happened to them but by what they are capable of right now. Van der Kolk advocates for therapeutic practices that help individuals not only to recount and process traumatic events but also to engage in activities that promote feelings of safety, mastery, and joy in the present. By doing so, therapy supports individuals in reclaiming control and pleasure in their lives, which is essential for a transformative healing experience.

When guiding women through healing trauma, I take them through two parallel journeys. One path addresses the traumatic experience in the past, and the other path helps them to live a meaningful and purposeful life in the moment. Bringing purpose to our pain and learning its spiritual lessons contributes to our healing of past, present, and future.

How can we encourage our clients to live fully in the present, strengthening their personal power, if we don't walk the talk? As professionals, it's crucial that we first embody the principles we advocate, living authentically and harnessing our personal power to inspire and empower those we serve truly.

> *Our role as healers is not only to clear the traces of past storms but also to encourage the growth of new, strong roots in the present.*

This approach goes beyond only coping or managing symptoms. It is about actively constructing a life that resonates with one's deepest values and attributes. In doing so, we guide our clients to survive and thrive. We offer them the tools to paint their lives with broad strokes of empowerment and purpose, transforming their narrative from trauma to triumph.

As Soulful Healers, we become more than healers; we become architects of hope. Together with our clients, we build a strong sense of self-worth and the ability to navigate life's changes. Our work goes beyond healing—it's a journey toward uncovering new possibilities and paths that lead to a fulfilling life.

As we embark on this sacred duty, we light the way for others to find their path, inspiring a ripple effect that can heal communities and the world.

> *By nurturing our personal power and guiding others to do the same, we transform healing into an art form—where values are the palette, attributes the brush strokes, and personal power the canvas on which we paint a future of wholeness and vibrant well-being.*

Now that we have explored the profound journey of healing, which involves embracing both our past and the present and the significance of embodying the values we hold dear, it is time to turn these insights into actionable steps.

Soulful Exercise:
Define Your Values and Attributes

1. Identify Your Personal Values:
   - Review the provided list of personal values. Trust your instinct and select your top 10 values.
   - Refine your list further by choosing your top 5 personal values.

2. Identify Your Professional Values:
   - Refer to the list of professional values. Again, rely on your intuition to pick your top 10 professional values.
   - Narrow down your list to your top 5 professional values.

3. Identify Your Attributes:
   - Review the list of attributes. Select the top 20 attributes that best describe your core self or who you aspire to be.
   - Then, trim down your list to your top 10 attributes.

4. Combine your chosen top values and attributes into one empowering statement. Engage with this statement daily.

Here is an example of an empowering statement created by one of the Soulful Healers in our community:

Here is what's important for me today:
Curiosity, harmony, joy, boldness, and balance.
[Her top personal values]
Authenticity, accountability, integrity, empathy, and boundaries.
[Her top professional values]
I am passionate. I am resilient. I am spiritual. I am a visionary.
[Her top attributes]
I am a Soulful Healer.

Another example of an empowering statement from a member of our Soulful Healers community:

Today, I prioritize these values in my life:
Exploration, peace, vitality, courage, and equilibrium.
[Her top personal values]
Sincerity, responsibility, honor, compassion, and limits.
[Her top professional values]
I am spirited. I am steadfast. I am insightful. I am an Innovator.
[Her top attributes]
I embody the essence of a Soulful Healer.

Another example of an empowering statement, written by one of the Soulful Healers in our community after engaging in inner work and reflection, is somewhat more expansive:

Here's what's important for me today:
To embody presence in the service to love.
Because compassion and kindness are the ultimate healers.
I vow to practice levity. To walk softly, uplift the negative, and continually commence with my inner childlike joy and wonder.
I vow to honor all things. Time, space, flow, the present. Deep respect for the now. Honoring the divinity and autonomy of others. The cycles of life. Myself, my limits, my gifts.
I vow to practice grace, to dance in the flow, to allow honor and love to flow through me and guide my actions.
Above all, I vow to practice faith, trust, and surrender in and to the organizational and abundant nature of the universe. Trust in knowing that G*d is conspiring to bring about my thought good and those of others around me.

Inventory Lists: Personal & Professional Values and Attributes

~ Personal Values ~

Growth

Self-improvement
Learning
Ambition
Curiosity

Open-mindedness
Determination
Adaptability
Wisdom

Personal development
Innovation

Selfhood

Self-love
Self-care
Self-respect

Self-esteem
Self-appreciation

Self-acceptance
Inner beauty

Happiness

Joyfulness
Contentment
Optimism
Pleasure

Cheerfulness
Gratitude
Positivity
Enjoyment

Satisfaction
Enthusiasm

Integrity

Honesty
Trustworthiness
Ethicality

Authenticity
Reliability
Responsibility

Fairness
Transparency
Consistency

Community

Cooperation
Supportiveness
Inclusivity

Social responsibility
Contribution
Altruism

Unity
Belonging
Solidarity

Resilience

Perseverance	Endurance	Courage
Toughness	Strength	Resourcefulness
Flexibility	Stability	
Recovery	Tenacity	

Well-being

Health	Relaxation	Harmony
Balance	Self-care	Mindfulness
Vitality	Safety	
Peace	Comfort	

Heartfulness

Compassion	Warmth	Love
Empathy	Generosity	Tenderness
Kindness	Care	Sincerity

Leadership

Influence	Visionary	Decisiveness
Direction	Initiative	Inspiration
Command	Authority	
Empowerment	Responsibility	

Creativity

Innovation	Inspiration	Unconventionality
Originality	Expression	Vision
Imagination	Ingenuity	

Spirituality

Faith	Devotion	Mysticism
Enlightenment	Sanctity	Sacredness
Transcendence	Reverence	
Inner peace	Grace	

Freedom

Independence	Free will	Self-expression
Autonomy	Choice	Spontaneity
Liberation	Flexibility	

Recreation

Fun	Leisure	Exploration
Playfulness	Relaxation	Movement
Adventure	Entertainment	Enjoyment

Awareness

Consciousness	Mindfulness	Recognition
Insight	Perception	Clarity
Understanding	Enlightenment	

Lifestyle

Simplicity	Tradition	Comfort
Elegance	Practicality	Convenience
Sophistication	Luxury	
Modernity	Minimalism	

Generosity

Altruism	Sharing	Bountifulness
Charity	Kind-heartedness	
Giving	Unselfishness	

~ *Professional Values* ~

Accountability
Adaptability
Advocacy
Altruism
Authenticity
Autonomy
Boundaries
Collaboration
Communication
Compassion
Competence
Confidentiality
Continuous learning
Cultural competence
Cultural sensitivity
Curiosity

Diversity
 and Inclusion
Empathy
Empowerment
Emotional
 intelligence
Equality
Ethical practice
Excellence
Flexibility
Honesty
Humility
Integrity
Non-judgment
Objectivity
Open-mindedness

Patience
Privacy
Professional ethics
Professionalism
Quality of care
Resilience
Respect
Responsibility
Self-care
Self-reflection
Social responsibility
Teamwork
Transparency
Trust building
Trustworthiness
Work–life balance

~ Attributes ~

Personal Growth

Ambitious	Wise	Adaptable
Curious	Innovative	Good learner
Open-minded	Self-motivated	Driven
Determined		

Positive Outlook

Happy	Pleasure-seeking	Positive
Joyful	Cheerful	Satisfied
Content	Grateful	Cheerful
Optimistic		

Integrity

Honest	Authentic	Fair
Trustworthy	Reliable	Transparent
Ethical	Responsible	Human

Community

Cooperative	Contributing	Engaged
Supportive	Belong	Giver
Friendly		

Resilience

Perseverant	Stable	Daring
Flexible	Tenacious	Courageous
Strong	Resourceful	Bold

Well-Being

Healthy	Relaxed	Harmonious
Balanced	Self-caring	Mindful
Vital	Safe	Zen-like
Peaceful	Comfortable	

Excellence

Achiever	Expert	Skillful
Masterful	Precise	Professional
Distinct	Great	

Heartfulness

Compassionate	Warm	Loving
Empathetic	Generous	Tender
Kind	Caring	

Creativity

Innovative	Inspired	Unconventional
Imaginative	Expressive	Visionary

Spirituality

Faithful	Peace-seeker	Poised
Enlightened	Devoted	Spiritual
Transcendent	Sacred	

Leadership

Influential	Visionary	Decisive
Directive	Responsible	Inspiring
Empowering		

Freedom

Independent	Free-willed	Self-expressive
Autonomous	Choice-making	Spontaneous
Liberated	Flexible	

Recreation

Fun-loving	Leisurely	Enjoying
Playful	Relaxed	Refreshed
Adventurous	Explorative	

Awareness

Insightful	Mindful	Clear
Understanding	Enlightened	Self-aware

Lifestyle

Simple	Modern	Luxurious
Elegant	Traditional	Minimalist
Sophisticated	Practical	Comfort-seeker

Generosity

Altruistic	Sharing	Unselfish
Giving	Kind-hearted	

Aesthetics

Beautiful	Elegant	Tasteful
Stylish		

To practically embody the empowerment explored in this chapter, join me in a guided visualization that's designed to illuminate your path toward aligning your values and attributes with your envisioned future as a Soulful Healer.

Guided Visualization:
Navigate the Sea of Possibilities

This guided visualization is designed to help you uncover your endless potential as a professional. It enhances self-awareness, reveals contrasts between your present and imagined future, inspires positive change, and fosters personal growth toward becoming a Soulful Healer.

When you are ready to begin the journey, find a comfortable position, take a deep breath, and listen to the instructions you've downloaded (which are transcribed below).

Take a deep breath and close your eyes.

And take one more breath to release any tension from your body.

Relax your body, relax your mind, calm your heart, and allow yourself to "be."

Imagine walking on a beautiful beach, feeling the warmth of the sun and the sand beneath your feet, and gazing out at the ocean's vastness.

You look around, and you notice that you are on an island. As you look around, you see images of your current life. Don't try to think of those images. Just let them naturally emerge.

- How do you take care of yourself?
- What brings you joy?
- How do you make an impact and contribute?
- How do you feel?

Now, shift your attention to your communities. Reflect on the types of communities you belong to and where you find support. Consider your work–life balance and what inspires you.

As you stand on the Island of Your Current Life, notice another island. Your curiosity is sparked, and you decide to swim toward it. The water clears and purifies your body as you swim, renewing and rejuvenating you.

When you reach the second island, you see a sign that reads "The Soulful Healers' Island." Excitement fills you as other Soulful Healers welcome you.

As you explore the island, you begin to see yourself a year from now—as a Soulful Healer. What do you see? Don't think of the answers; just let those images naturally emerge. And if nothing comes up, stay curious and present in the experience.

What do you see on this second island a year from now once you become a Soulful Healer?

- How do you take care of yourself?
- What do you enjoy?
- What brings you joy?
- How do you make an impact and contribute?
- Notice any differences from your current life.

Observe your facial expressions and energy.

Consider your environment, who you work with, and the lifestyle you lead. Is there anything that surprises you about yourself on the Soulful Healers Island?

Before leaving this island of endless possibilities, look around and notice any additional details.

While looking around, a bird lands nearby, carrying a note similar to the sign you saw before. Open the note and read the message of support. Accept it, whether a word, sentence, color, image, or feeling.

Thank the bird for its message and take one last look around. It's time to return to the Island of Your Current Life.

As you swim back, pay attention to how you feel during the journey.

Upon arriving at the Island of Your Current Life, pause and take in your surroundings. Notice how it feels to be back. Notice if there is any gap between the second island and the first island; if there is any tension, accept it.

Look back at the island of endless possibilities, The Soulful Healers Island. Take another minute to see if any further insights arise.

When you're ready, take a deep breath and open your eyes.

After the Visualization

After the visualization, while the vivid imagery of The Soulful Healers Island of Possibilities is still alive in your senses, take a moment to anchor these insights. Use the provided illustration of the islands as a canvas for your reflections. On this visual map, write down the information that came up during the visualization.

Allow your thoughts and feelings to flow onto the illustration, turning it into a personalized map of your professional aspirations and inner discoveries. This creative act bridges the gap between intangible experiences and concrete expressions, making your journey toward becoming a Soulful Healer both visible and tangible.

Keep this illustrated map in a place where you can see it often. Let it remind you of the possibilities that lie within you and the path you are carving out for yourself as a professional. When you revisit this map, add new insights or goals as you continue to evolve, allowing it to be a living document of your journey toward empowerment and healing.

Reflect on the Chapter: Questions to Consider

1. How do your professional values complement or align with your personal values?

2. In which areas, if any, do your personal and professional values conflict? How can you navigate these conflicts?

3. Reflect on your childhood attributes. How have they evolved over time, and how are they manifested in your personal and professional life today?

4. Out of the list of attributes that reflect your core self, which ones do you feel most connected to now compared to the past? Which ones would you like to develop or connect with more deeply in the future?

5. Consider your professional persona. Are the attributes that define you personally the same as those you express professionally? If not, what are the differences?

From Words to Action: Applying This Chapter's Lessons

▸ Embark on the transformative journey outlined in this chapter by engaging with the exercises to identify your core values and attributes.

▸ And here's a creative idea: Combine your top values and attributes into a personal empowering statement that resonates with your *Soulful Healer identity*.

▸ Write the statement on an index card or sticky note and place it somewhere you will see it often—a bathroom mirror, your workspace, or your phone's wallpaper, so you can integrate reading the statement into your daily life.

▶ Start each morning by reciting this statement, allowing it to set the intention for your day, and let it serve as a constant reminder of your personal and professional commitment.

▶ By making it a living part of your routine, you affirm your dedication to growth, authenticity, and empowerment. *This daily practice isn't just a repetition of words but a step toward actualizing the soulful life you envision, creating a bridge between your current self and the empowered healer you are becoming.*

In the words of Lisa, one of the incredible healers trained to become a Soulful Healer: "Defining my values and attributes and creating my Empowerment Statement is like having a built-in board of ethics, coach, and cheerleader. And when one works this system, the result is an inner power formed through intelligent and intentional thought and action. As a Soulful Healer, this keeps me grounded in my "why" and directs my "how." It ignites an inner flame and teaches me how to use it to share my unique gifts with humanity best."

Unfolding the Next Layer

In this chapter, we've journeyed through the essence of empowerment, exploring the anchoring role of personal, professional, and collective values alongside the unique attributes that constitute our personal power.

This exploration is more than an academic exercise; it's a call to action, urging us to embody the principles that lead to a fulfilled life and a successful practice as a Soulful Healer. By connecting to our chosen values and attributes, not those pushed upon us by society or inherited from others, we craft a resilient core that enables us to face life's challenges and guide others with authenticity and confidence.

The exercises and reflections are designed to bring these concepts into sharp focus and transform them into daily practices that reinforce our commitment to growth and service. We create a powerful synergy that drives us forward as we align our actions with our values and infuse our daily routines with our empowering statement. This synergy enhances our well-being, elevates our professional practice, and magnifies our impact on the world

Through this process, we use the full spectrum of our personal power, leading us to a path of continuous development, joyous service, and profound healing—for ourselves and those we are privileged to serve.

> Navigating the immense responsibilities of our personal power can sometimes feel overwhelming, yet we are not meant to shoulder this journey alone. We must also rely on a different kind of power that lightens our burdens and wraps us in the sense of profound support, ensuring that we are uplifted and sustained as we continue to empower ourselves and others.

In the next chapter, we'll investigate a partnership with this bigger power.

Chapter 2
KEY # 2—SPIRITUALITY
We Are Part of
Something Bigger

Before You Begin, Download These Resources:

"Spiritual Alignment" guided visualization audio and the "Map of Spirituality" in color.

https://beaconout.com/bsr

A s the sun rises over a busy Indian city, it casts a golden hue on the faces of its inhabitants, rich and poor alike. The sounds of laughter, honking rickshaws, and street vendors fill the air. In the kaleidoscope of life, where fancy houses stand next to simple shacks, it's hard not to see the significant gaps in wealth. Yet, an underlying sense of unity and contentment transcends these material differences. Despite their struggles and hardships, the poor show a profound resilience and strength, their smiles reflecting an unwavering hope for a better future.

During my trip to India many years ago, I first glimpsed the essence of true spirituality as I witnessed first-hand the remarkable ability of the human spirit to find happiness and meaning in the face of adversity.

In the midst of this vibrant chaos, I formed bonds with local women whose lives were steeped in simplicity, yet they radiated an inner joy that seemed unshaken by their circumstances. I was invited to weddings and festive holiday gatherings, where the air buzzed with joy and a profound sense of sacredness. These celebrations were less about material abundance and more about the rich spirit of community. They shared hope that brought everyone together, creating a joy-filled experience that transcended their economic status.

And while many people find India's poverty depressing, I felt different. Instead of sadness, I was struck by awe and inspiration. Witnessing the incredible strength and resilience of those living in difficult conditions, I realized that happiness is not solely determined by material wealth or circumstances. With their unwavering spirit, these individuals taught me that true contentment comes from within and that, even in the face of adversity, one can find joy and meaning in life. This realization transformed my perspective, allowing me to embark on a spiritual journey that shaped my understanding of what truly matters.

Over the years, my spiritual journey has evolved and taken various forms. From exploring kundalini meditation in Germany and practicing Zen meditation in Israel, to participating in and leading classes, workshops, and spiritual retreats in the U.S., I've had the privilege of meeting incredible teachers and students. These experiences have shaped me into both a spiritual mentor and a lifelong learner. After all, discovering and embracing spiritual lessons is a never-ending adventure that continues throughout our lives.

Spirituality, as a key to becoming a Soulful Healer, is essential because it captures the complete range of our existence, merging our everyday experiences with the practice of tapping into something that is bigger than us. In this chapter on spirituality, I have set the stage for a profound understanding that our Human Self and our Divine Self are not separate; instead, they are complementary aspects of our being.

> *Our physical existence and our spiritual essence are two halves of a whole, constantly in dialogue and in dance with each other, influencing and enriching our journey through life. This key to spirituality is embracing the full spectrum of who we are—recognizing that our day-to-day lives are the ground on which our spiritual selves walk.*

Understanding Spirituality: The Unseen Thread of Connection

> *Imagine spirituality as the silent partner to everything we do, feel, and think. It's not a complicated set of rules or ideas we have to follow; instead, it's like the air we breathe—so essential that without it, we feel incomplete.*

To understand spirituality, we must first acknowledge what it is not. It is not the hollow echo of inner emptiness nor the persistent pursuit to fill a void. It's not about turning away from the part of us that yearns for deeper meaning. Nor is it a destination reached by following a prescribed set of rules or a path walked with the crutch of dependency.

> *Spirituality is a gentle yet powerful force, the essence of creation and existence that flows through us, infusing our lives with meaning and guiding us forward. Spirituality is in the big, wide universe and every part of our everyday lives.*

Regardless of the name we give it—God, Higher Power, Higher Self, Source Energy, Universe, Universal Energy, Spirit, Life-Force Energy, Creation Force—*embracing spirituality means recognizing our connection to a power that is greater than us.*

Without a spiritual connection, we feel like a boat without a paddle, drifting without direction. But when we embrace our spiritual side, we find our way, which doesn't rely on anyone else's map.

Spirituality also extends to our relationships with others, the world around us, our personal power, and a power greater than ourselves. This profound bond must be firmly rooted in universal values such as love, freedom, unity, and personal growth.

Soulful Snapshot

Consider the journey of Jenn, a dedicated massage therapist, Reiki Master, and member of the Soulful Healer community. From a young age, Jenn experienced a profound connection to a greater force that guided and protected her. This connection wasn't tied to the religious beliefs she was raised with, prompting intense inner work, spiritual work, and soul-searching. It wasn't until her mid-40s that Jenn truly embraced her truth, prompting her to leave the suffocating confines of corporate America and the toxic negativity that infused her environment.

She was empowered to make the leap by the realization that leaving a toxic environment was aligned with her chosen values and the trust in guidance from something greater than herself. In doing so, Jenn liberated herself from the restrictive beliefs imposed by organized religion and society's expectations that she grew up with. In this process, she discovered her true calling. She may not have known then, but this decision would eventually lead to a profound connection with her purpose.

As a massage therapist, she found a profound sense of fulfillment in the healing touch, the transfer of energy, and the deep compassion involved in her work. Serving others in this way resonated with her spiritual path and felt like coming home—a clear manifestation of her spiritual beliefs guiding her to her life's work. Her story is a testament to the transformative power of aligning one's career with one's inner truth, revealed through a spiritual journey.

> *Maintaining a spiritual connection empowers us to tap into the vast pool of awareness, insights, abstract notions, and inspirations from the boundless ocean of cosmic consciousness, transforming them into tangible elements within our daily lives in the material world.*

The Dance of the Divine and Human Selves

An individual's inner world embraces a variety of parts and elements, including the Human and Divine Selves.

> *Our Divine Self embodies the elevated dimension of cosmic consciousness. Our Human Self represents the human consciousness and the material world.*

Imagine you're gazing at the night sky and you're suddenly filled with a profound sense of connection to the universe. An idea sparks within you—for example, a vision of starting a community garden that feeds the body and nourishes the Soul, promoting well-being and unity among people. This inspiration is the voice of your Divine Self, tapping into the elevated dimension of cosmic consciousness. It provides the grand vision, the sense of purpose, and the recognition of interconnectedness that transcends the everyday.

Then, your Human Self steps in—the part of you that lives in the tangible, material world. It begins to map out the practical steps needed to bring this vision into reality. You start researching the best plants for the local climate, contacting community members for support, gathering materials, and planning the garden layout.

Your Human Self translates the lofty idea from your spiritual awareness into actionable tasks. It considers the logistics, the physical effort, and the day-to-day activities required to manifest the dream. This duality of self—the Divine and the Human—works in harmony to create something that reflects the beauty of the universe and the tangible reality of our world.

> *In the dance of existence, spirituality forms the bridge between our Divine and Human selves, translating cosmic possibilities into everyday actions.*

The Next Element in Our Spiritual Exploration: The Soul

As we delve deeper into the world of spirituality, we turn our attention to another essential element: The Soul.

> *Nestled within our spiritual core, the Soul holds our divine potential. She carries the guiding spark that helps us embrace the connection between heaven and earth, cosmic and human consciousness.*

The Soul is like a wise friend within us, softly nudging us along our life's path.

It speaks in the quiet of intuition, in the symbols of dreams, and in those "aha" moments when everything just clicks into place. It's the inner voice that whispers wisdom, helping us to choose paths that are true to who we are at heart.

Our *Soul Signature* is our personal essence, a unique mix of what we love, what we believe in, and the personal touch we bring to our actions. It's like a fingerprint of the spirit; no two are the same. It's the mark we leave on every task we undertake, every relationship we nurture, and every choice we make. It's our unique expression in the world. Our Soul Signature is the energy we radiate, and the unspoken essence that others feel from us. When we live in harmony with our Soul Signature, our lives become a true expression of our innermost self.

Lauren, a Soulful Healer, described her transformative experience of reconnecting with her soul: "The insight key where we claimed our soulfulness was SO HUGE for me. To really own and put into words my unique soul expression was transformative. Initially, I wrote about what I do, but then we were encouraged to write about who we are—our unique soul expression. I realized that the soul doesn't "do," it simply "is"—and that was so powerful for me. Understanding, writing, and owning my unique expression was one of the training's most powerful and empowering moments. Doing this alongside other Soulful Healers made it even more impactful. I'm still integrating this experience, and I believe it was a huge part of my personal and professional development."

The Soul is where our true self lives, pulsing with the energy of life. It's the living core of our being, filled with our feelings, experiences, life stories, and treasured memories, all of which chart the course of our evolution and the essence of our being. Our Soul maps out where we've been and where we're headed, shaping who we are.

By nurturing our Soul, we strengthen our connection to the divine and ultimately unlock the boundless potential within our human and spiritual selves. Part of Soul nourishment is embracing the entire spectrum of our emotions and experiences.

" Our Soul yearns to experience the fullness of the human condition, accepting the joys and challenges. It acknowledges that suffering and comfort, fear and bravery, despair, and hope are vital to our life's mosaic. "

Expanding Our Journey: The Pathways of Spiritual Channels

Before we continue to explore the Soul's pivotal role in our inner universe through the next chapter of this book, let's shift our focus to the *Spiritual Channels* through which we connect and practice spirituality.

While spirituality might seem elusive, it becomes tangible and meaningful when actively participating in activities designed to enhance it. These activities, known as Spiritual Channels, provide us with concrete ways to apply spiritual concepts to our daily lives, leading to personal growth and deep inner change.

These channels are necessary for nurturing our spiritual health, just like exercising is necessary to keep our bodies healthy. Through practices such as meditation, prayer, yoga, acts of kindness, and journaling, to name a few, we maintain and develop our spiritual fitness, fostering a sense of harmony within ourselves and with the world around us.

Spending time connecting with nature, participating in energy healing, or exploring sacred rituals can open doors to profound experiences, easing our burdens and balancing our emotions. They provide us with tools to tap into the heart of our existence, exploring and understanding the vast landscape of our inner lives.

Incorporating these practices into our daily lives can lead to a significant shift in perspective, helping us to find calm in the chaos, and clarity in confusion. They offer us a steady foundation, especially in tumultuous times, granting us access to a state of being aligned with our true essence and purpose.

" Spirituality can often feel abstract or vague until we engage in specific practices that bring it into focus. Spiritual Channels are activities that ground our spirituality in practical experience, helping us to grow personally and transform from the inside out. "

The Final Element: Expression Channels

As we deepen our engagement with our Soul, and cross through Spiritual Channels, our capacity to manifest these profound experiences into the world through diverse forms of expression naturally expands.

While Spiritual Channels allow us to cultivate our inner spirituality, it is through *Expression Channels* that we give voice to these internal transformations, making spirituality an active and visible force in our lives.

Expression Channels are how the intangible aspects of our spirituality become concrete actions and contributions in the world. They are the external manifestations of the inner growth and insights we gain from our spiritual practices. While Spiritual Channels are personal and often private actions, Expression Channels are public and interpersonal, involving sharing our spiritual essence with others and the world.

For instance, consider acts of kindness. Privately, one might cultivate compassion and empathy as a spiritual practice. The Expression Channel of this could be performing tangible acts of service, such as bringing food to a sick neighbor. This action extends the internal cultivation of kindness into a physical expression that benefits others.

Another example is a daily practice like Reiki, my primary spiritual practice since 1996. When practiced alone, it serves as a Spiritual Channel for personal energy healing and balance. However, when I offer Reiki sessions to others or teach it, this becomes an Expression

Channel. It's about taking the personal spiritual benefit and turning it into a shared experience or service.

Medical professionals, for example, may view their work as an Expression Channel. Their expertise and care in treating patients become the physical manifestation of their spiritual desire to heal and serve humanity. Similarly, a singer might use their voice and performances as an Expression Channel, bringing their audience joy, inspiration, or comfort through their art.

I love how Madeleine, a Soulful Healer, defined Expressions Channels as an "inside-out flow of your gifts."

> In the symphony of the Soulful Healer's life, Expression Channels are our instruments, amplifying the silent music of our Souls into a harmony that resonates in the world, and turning our spiritual growth into meaningful actions and contributions that serve others.

Putting It All Together: The Human and Divine Map of Spirituality

Having journeyed through the various aspects of spirituality, including the Human and Divine Selves, the depths of our Souls, the pathways of Spiritual Channels, and the transformative power of Expression Channels, we now stand on the edge of a profound revelation. It's time to unite these elements into a single inspiring vision—a map guiding us through the complex territory of our inner and outer worlds. Welcome to *The Human and Divine Map of Spirituality*, where the threads of our spiritual journey create a masterpiece reflecting our essence and cosmic connection.

   The Human and Divine Map of Spirituality weaves the Soul's vibrancy with our dual selves and the countless pathways of our spiritual practice. It serves as a vivid framework, illustrating how we may journey through the Spiritual Channels that nurture our inner being and express our profound connections outwardly.

THE HUMAN AND DIVINE MAP OF SPIRITUALITY

DIVINE SELF

Spiritual
Channels

Soul

Expression
Channels

HUMAN SELF

Spiritual Diversity and Warning Signs

There are infinite spiritual paths, each providing unique ways for individuals to journey from their souls toward higher levels of awareness.

However, there are instances where spiritual guidance is misused. Some leaders or communities may impose rigid rules, transforming spirituality into a constraining practice that represses personal choice. Such restrictions can prevent individuals from embracing spirituality in a way that genuinely empowers their uniqueness and authenticity.

Common misconceptions about spirituality can obscure its true essence. It is often mistakenly believed that spirituality necessitates a retreat from worldly matters, hindering one's ability to remain present and grounded in daily life. Additionally, the false notion persists that spirituality is about following restrictive rules that limit personal freedom. Adding to the confusion is how often people mix up spirituality with religion, thinking that following certain religious practices is the same as having spiritual guidance. These misconceptions can create barriers to appreciating spirituality as a deeply personal and expansive journey that stands apart from religious dogma.

> *For spirituality to be a positive, supportive aspect of one's life, the spiritual journey should embody a dynamic, expansive, adaptable, and open process that challenges conventional thinking and fosters continuous growth and nurturing for the Soul.*

Our responsibility is to identify spiritual teachings that impose limitations due to strict expectations and rules followers must obey. When such teachings create dependency and demand compliance with a rigid set of guidelines that lack openness or flexibility for growth, change, and modification, it serves as a warning sign that this spiritual teaching is not aligned with universal values of love, kindness, compassion, unity, and personal development.

As professionals, we are also responsible for self-reflecting and evaluating when we use spirituality with ourselves or our clients to bypass and avoid dealing with unaddressed emotions and trauma.

> *Supportive, nurturing spirituality should encourage growth, independence, freedom, and open-mindedness, and we must watch for signs of rigid teachings or spiritual bypassing.*

Why Every Professional Must Cultivate a Strong Spiritual Foundation

Our core values and personal strengths empower us as professionals, infusing confidence and a sense of self-worth. However, an exclusive reliance on personal power can lead to an imbalance: Becoming an overachiever, an excessive fixer, or someone who assumes too much responsibility, which can be burdensome. Arianna Huffington, the co-founder of *The Huffington Post* and a renowned author on well-being and productivity, always says that life involves a blend of making things happen and letting them happen.

> *True equilibrium is found when we share our burdens with a force greater than ourselves, easing into the role of co-creators. It's about forming a symbiotic relationship with the essence of life or a higher power, engaging with the profound process of co-creation.*

Picture this: During a session, your client shows a level of resistance that usually doesn't discourage you, thanks to your professional expertise. However, this time it sends you into a downward spiral of self-doubt and imposter syndrome. As you feel overwhelmed, a realization dawns on you: You are not in this alone. There's no need for your Human Self to shoulder the burden solo. You call upon your Divine Self, drawing from your Spiritual Channels, and allow yourself to relax into the process. This new level of calmness broadens your perspective, offering clarity and awakening your inner guidance. Your intuition becomes a guiding light. Empowered by this harmonious blend of personal strength, professional knowledge, and spiritual insight, you navigate your client through the session with renewed confidence and wisdom.

Is it possible to excel as a therapist, life coach, or healing professional without spirituality? Indeed, one can be an outstanding professional without engaging with spirituality. Yet, by not incorporating a spiritual foundation, you may overlook the profound depth of your potential and the Soul's deeper calling.

A solid spiritual connection provides extraordinary resources for alleviating suffering, sustaining personal health and peace, and cultivating a distinctive presence in a field abundant with helpers. Embracing this dimension can significantly enrich your impact and fulfillment in your industry.

You might question the validity of my perspective—that spirituality is essential for Soulful Healers. You might wonder, what are the challenges for professionals who lack a solid spiritual foundation?

When lacking a spiritual dimension, professionals may experience unique challenges. Without the perspective and resources that spirituality provides, it becomes easy to feel the weight of responsibility for clients' progress. This burden can lead to burnout, a sense of isolation in the struggle for client breakthroughs, and a vulnerability to compassion fatigue.

They are relying solely on their Human Self, and on the clinical techniques and strategies, which, while effective, might miss the subtler cues and deeper healing opportunities that a spiritually attuned approach could reveal.

Moreover, the absence of a spiritual framework can limit your ability to fully connect with clients on an emotional and existential level. It may also restrict your own personal growth, as the spiritual aspects of healing often invite therapists and coaches to evolve alongside their clients. Without this growth, you risk stagnation, both in your practice and personal life.

Growing up in a household where spirituality was not encouraged, and bearing the limiting beliefs against religion taught by my environment, I had little reason to develop a spiritual connection. Yet, it was through my own trauma and wounds that I found comfort in spirituality, distinct from religious practice. Discovering Reiki in 1996 marked a turning point in both my personal and professional lives. My routine of daily self-treatment began as a means of healing and evolved into a spiritual practice. It provided a means to lighten the load and responsibility that often emerge when helping others heal. Reiki offered me a concrete method to engage with both my Human and Divine Selves, to access my personal and spiritual power, ensuring I am supported in my service to others. This dual connection has been instrumental in helping me balance the active pursuit of making things happen with the receptiveness of letting things happen.

Learning to tune into the Divine and Human Selves and the Soul allows us to receive higher guidance and a broader perspective and to see endless ways to solve any problem.

Maintaining a solid spiritual foundation also enhances your dual role as participant and observer. It enables you to remain engaged without getting entangled in the narratives or dramas clients may present. Spirituality provides the clarity to step back neutrally, offering the objectivity and perspective needed to discover the spiritual lesson we are meant to learn.

As we navigate the rich world of spirituality, it's crucial to remain cautious against spiritual bypassing—a tendency to use spiritual ideas or practices to sidestep or avoid facing unresolved emotional issues, psychological wounds, and unfinished developmental tasks. This often involves overlaying a kind of spiritual correctness or idealism on top of complex life situations without addressing the fundamental human needs at their core.

> *Integrating spirituality into our professional journey is transformative, granting us the vision to see beyond the surface. It brings a depth of perspective that lights up our path, helping us to balance personal drive with the wisdom of co-creation.*

Soulful Exercise:
Exploring Your Personal Map of Spirituality

To help you gain clarity around your own Human and Divine Map of Spirituality, take some time to go through the following exercise.

Step 1: Reflect on Your Spiritual Journey

Take some time to reflect on your spiritual journey so far. Consider the experiences, beliefs, practices, and teachings that have influenced and shaped your spirituality.

Write down significant moments or milestones that have brought you closer to understanding your connection with the divine.

Step 2: Identify Your Spiritual Channels

List activities, practices, or rituals that have helped you nurture your spiritual connection. These are your Spiritual Channels.

Think about the ones that resonate most with you and have brought you peace, joy, or spiritual growth.

Note down as many Spiritual Channels as come to mind.

For inspiration, here are some examples of Spiritual Channels:

- meditative practices like meditation, prayer, mindfulness, and yoga
- cultivating compassion and empathy
- reflective exercises, including journaling and studying spiritual texts

- ❧ connecting with the earth through nature immersion and eco-spirituality
- ❧ healing modalities, like energy work and sacred ceremonies
- ❧ expression through chanting, music, or creative arts
- ❧ transformative techniques such as breathwork, visualization, or manifestation

Step 3: Reflect on Your Expression Channels

Consider how you express your spirituality in the world and how you use it to serve others. Reflect on your unique talents, passions, and skills and how they align with your spiritual beliefs.

Write down how you bring the higher dimension's abstract information into your life and contribute to humanity's collective growth and evolution.

Examples of Expression Channels:

- ❧ medical professionals and therapists healing and treating others
- ❧ artists like singers, painters, and writers channeling creativity
- ❧ spiritual teachers and mentors sharing wisdom
- ❧ activists engaging in social justice
- ❧ coaches guiding on spiritual journeys
- ❧ counselors offering guidance
- ❧ technologists broadcasting spiritual messages
- ❧ volunteers serving communities
- ❧ entrepreneurs infusing businesses with spiritual intent
- ❧ creating sacred spaces
- ❧ acts of kindness and community service
- ❧ environmental advocacy
- ❧ leading workshops or retreats
- ❧ leading spiritual organizations

Step 4: Assess Alignment and Growth

Review your lists of Spiritual Channels and Expression Channels. Reflect on whether these channels align with your personal, professional, and collective values and the attributes you have identified in Chapter 1.

Consider how they have supported your personal growth and spiritual development.

Identify areas where you feel called to explore new avenues or deepen your existing practices.

Step 5: Set Intentions for Integration

Based on your reflection, set intentions for consciously integrating your Spiritual Channels and Expression Channels into your daily life. This could involve committing to regular practice, exploring new avenues for growth, or finding ways to align your passions and talents with your spiritual journey.

Write down your intentions and any action steps you can execute.

Step 6: Revisit and Revise

As you continue your spiritual journey, revisit and revise your Human and Divine Map of Spirituality periodically.

Allow yourself the flexibility to explore new practices, refine existing ones, and adapt to the ever-evolving nature of your spiritual path.

If you practice any religious practices, you can choose to integrate them into your map.

Embarking on a spiritual journey often involves a deep inner transformation. As we transition from exploring the ongoing dance between our Human and Divine Selves, let's engage with a guided visualization to harmonize these aspects within us. This practice is an invitation to deepen your connection with your spiritual essence and embody the profound realizations from this chapter.

Guided Visualization: Spiritual Alignment

This guided visualization is designed to harmonize the spiritual and earthly elements of our being. Through this process, we aim to activate the third eye Chakra, encouraging deep internal reflection and a connection with the Soul's light, which purifies and balances our inner landscape.

When you are ready to begin the journey, find a comfortable position, take a deep breath, and listen to the audio you've downloaded, which is transcribed below.

Take a few deep breaths. Allow your breath to become your anchor, grounding you in the present moment.

Pay attention to the pause between each breath as you inhale and exhale.

Bring your awareness to the middle of your forehead, where the third eye Chakra is located. This is "the eye between the eyes," which allows us to look within.

Imagine a spiral of light opening up your third eye area. As you breathe, allow your internal eye to guide you in, looking within yourself. Visualize a tiny spark of light nestled in the center of your body, where your Soul lives.

With each breath, imagine this spark of light growing and expanding. Feel it radiating beams of light, extending up and down through your spiritual conduit—the channel that connects heaven and earth and your Human and Divine Selves.

From the depths of your Soul, these beams of light send pure energy and unconditional love up and down, clearing and purifying your spiritual vessel. The light carries a powerful energy, cleansing and purifying the channel.

Allow this pure positive energy and unconditional love to flow freely, connecting your Divine and Human Selves. Embrace the harmony that emerges as you connect your spiritual and earthly aspects. Notice if there is a sense of integration and alignment within yourself.

As you inhale, gently press the lower part of your body down, deepening your connection with the earth beneath you. Feel yourself rooting down, grounding yourself in the energy of Mother Earth. At the same time, straighten your spine and lengthen your upper body upwards, reaching toward the divine. This dual movement strengthens your vertical connection, anchoring you between heaven and earth.

As you breathe, visualize the spark of light within your Soul, illuminating the path downwards and upwards. Embody this grounding posture, allowing it to bring awareness to your emotions. Take a moment to notice how you feel, without judgment or criticism. Approach your feelings with compassion and mindfulness, acknowledging them for what they are.

Be present with your feelings, honoring their presence within you. Give yourself permission to fully experience and embrace your emotions, knowing they are a natural part of your human experience. Treat yourself with kindness and understanding as you navigate your inner landscape.

As you root down and connect with the earth and stretch upwards toward the divine, you are creating harmony and balance within yourself.

Take a few more moments to breathe deeply and bask in the loving energy flowing through you. When you're ready, gently bring your awareness back to the present moment, carrying the sense of connection you've cultivated with you.

Reflect on the Chapter:
Questions to Consider

1. How has your understanding of spirituality evolved over time? What specific experiences or practices have shaped this evolution?

2. In what ways do you integrate spirituality into your daily life? How does this integration affect your sense of purpose and direction?

3. Reflect on the concept of Spiritual Channels. Which practices have you found most beneficial in nurturing your spiritual health?

4. Considering Expression Channels, how do you or could you manifest your spirituality in actions that serve others?

5. Moving forward, how do you plan to explore or deepen your connection with your Divine and Human Selves?

From Words to Action:
Applying This Chapter's Lessons

▶ Create your Human and Divine Map of Spirituality: Begin by completing the steps outlined in this chapter. Reflect on your spiritual journey, identify your Spiritual Channels, understand your Expression Channels, and set intentions for integrating these channels with everyday life.

▶ Once you've crafted your Map of Spirituality, consider placing it in a visible and sacred space in your environment, such as your meditation corner or workspace. This serves as a daily reminder of your spiritual path.

▶ Regularly practice the guided visualization. Set aside a few minutes each day to practice this visualization. It can help you stay grounded, connect to your spirituality, and maintain a balance in your life.

▶ Engage in open and meaningful conversations with like-minded individuals who are open to exploring spirituality. Join spiritual groups or communities where you can share your experiences, learn from others, and be curious and open-minded in exploring further the spiritual aspects presented in this chapter. Sit with the questions and engage in discussions that allow you to deepen your understanding of spirituality, providing valuable insights and expanding your spiritual horizons.

Soulful Snapshot

To give a real-life example of a Soulful Healer who embodies her Map of Spirituality, here's how Lauren described her transformative experience with the Human and Divine Map of Spirituality.

Lauren is an ashitasu therapist, Reiki practitioner, hypnotist and a participant in the Soulful Healer program. Embracing the first key, empowerment, she rediscovered her core personal and professional values, which reaffirmed her capabilities.

Then came the second key, with the Map of Spirituality. Lauren connected with the map and embodied it daily as a reminder to remain grounded. She describes a sacred connection, extending her heart upwards to the divine and downwards into the earth, connecting her Human and Divine Selves, a duality that now makes her feel whole.

The concept of Expression Channels resonated deeply with Lauren, providing a structured approach to serve others effectively. Where once she struggled with professional burnout, she now enjoys a mindset and feeling of vitality and empowerment. She created a shift in perspective; she no longer fixates on session outcomes but focuses on being fully present and connected. This profound internal shift has ignited her inner flame and manifested outwardly, attracting more clients and increasing her income.

Lauren attributes this success to her newfound inner spark, driving her practice toward the highest good for her clients. "By harmonizing divine and cosmic consciousness through my Soul," says Lauren, "I enhance its expression in daily life. Grounded in my unique earthly signature, I contribute to humanity's evolution as guided by my Soul's wisdom."

Unfolding the Next Layer

Recall the invitation I offered at the beginning of this book, where I encouraged you to seek clarity on a missing element—a mysterious aspect that could add greater depth to your practice. As you delve into my perspective on spirituality, might it be that this elusive piece has become more concrete? Could spirituality indeed be that missing piece?

In this chapter, we covered the fundamental truth that happiness and fulfillment are not dependent upon material wealth but are found within one's inner life. The narratives of strength and hope emerging from the bustling streets of India serve as a testament to the boundless nature of the human Soul, capable of transcending the most daunting of circumstances through spirituality.

Spirituality is presented not as a lofty, inaccessible concept but as a core, universal aspect of our existence, similar to the air we breathe. It's about finding harmony in the union of our Divine and Human Selves, where inspiration drawn from the cosmos translates into actionable reality. This synergy animates the human experience, empowering us to navigate life with purpose, direction, and connection to something greater than ourselves.

The chapter also guided us through the gentle dance of our spiritual and human parts, emphasizing the continuous and dynamic interplay between the elevated dimensions of cosmic consciousness and the practicalities of the material world.

It is through this dance that we can embrace our spirituality in everyday life, finding joy and meaning in both the magnificence of the universe and the details of daily existence. This holistic approach to spirituality fosters personal growth, strengthens our relationships, and enables us to contribute positively to the world around us.

Can spirituality sometimes misguide us?

As with any profound aspect of human experience, spirituality holds the potential for misguidance if it is misunderstood or misapplied.

> *Spirituality is deeply personal, and what may serve as guidance for one might not suit another. Misguidance can occur when we adopt practices that lack personal significance, lose balance by relying solely on spirituality, or become isolated from others. It can also lead us in the wrong direction when we use spiritual bypassing to avoid confronting emotional issues or psychological wounds.*

What, then, is our safeguard? It is our Inner and Collective Wisdom that lives within our Soul. The Soul's discerning power acts as our protector, ensuring the spiritual guidance we follow resonates with our deepest truths. In the next chapter, we'll explore the art of tuning into the Soul, empowering you to align with your core essence.

Chapter 3
Key # 3—AUTHENTICITY
Nurturing a Connection with the Soul

Before You Begin, Download These Resources:

"Reconnect with Your Soul" guided visualization audio and the "Wheel of Soulful Living" in color.

https://beaconout.com/bsr

C overed in a relentless rash that itched with the fury of a thousand fires, Mika sought my help, desperate to reclaim the life that hives had hijacked. Despite seeking help from several specialists, including a dermatologist, she found no satisfactory resolution for her skin condition. I recommended she undertake the Journey into the Soul to uncover the root cause of her physical ailment.

I guided Mika through a visualization exercise to establish a deeper connection with her Soul during this process. As part of this exercise, we engaged in inner child work, where I periodically prompted her to ask questions about her Soul and listened attentively to the responses. Her Soul led her to connect with her inner child, a little girl whom she visualized playing outdoors in nature and dressed in a white dress her mother made for her when she was 10.

As the exercise progressed, Mika felt guided by her Soul to rub her hands. While doing so, she realized that the little girl in a white dress represented both her and her mother. She also saw another little child in her visualization. I steered her to observe a conversation between these two children as she continued to rub her hands. Mika realized that the little boy was her father, and he was there to love and protect her.

In my grounded and centered state, I allowed life-force energy to flow through me to Mika, enabling me to receive higher guidance. This led me to pose a few questions to Mika's mother's inner child, which revealed a forgotten memory: Her mother had suffered from rheumatism in her hands.

As Mika continued to rub her hands during the visualization, I sensed a shift in energy and profound healing taking place. The sacred space we co-created, combining our alignment with life-force energy and the Soul, provided her the safety to delve into deeper emotional layers. In this protected space, her previously unconscious emotions could emerge into awareness for healing and resolution.

Upon completing the session, Mika shared an intriguing observation. She felt that rubbing her hands had somehow initiated a healing process for her hives. Moreover, she believed this healing was connected to her mother's rheumatism, an understanding she never had before. We came to an astonishing realization that Mika's skin condition might have an unconscious link to her mother's health issues.

Although her mother had passed away four years before our session, the mother–daughter connection seemed to transcend the boundaries of the physical world, as if her mother's spirit were guiding Mika toward relief and comfort.

When I met Mika for a follow-up session a few weeks later, she told me that the skin rash was gone, the hives had almost cleared, and they did not bother her at all.

Mika's experience was not an isolated occurrence but rather a profound example of generational healing guided by the wisdom of the Soul—both mine and the client's.

The Soul's Medicine: Infusing Daily Life with Sacredness

We've all felt a sense of emptiness sometimes, as though something within us is absent. This void can result from traumatic events, personal crises, global disasters, or significant life changes, leading to a detachment from our Souls.

Looking back at your own life, can you identify those moments—a significant crisis, a transition, or a life challenge—that left you feeling depressed? Could there be the times you were disconnected from your Soul?

Now, put on your professional hat. Many practitioners are well versed in the complex dance between physical ailments and emotional states, recognizing that often, our physical distress has emotional roots. No one in our profession takes lightly seeing a distressed client; instead, we are united by a shared drive to foster profound healing.

In our quest, Soulful Healers go beyond the standard arsenal of breathing exercises and mindfulness practices. We are committed to finding methods that ignite healing from within, tapping into the deepest wellsprings of wellness.

Think back to moments when you've been burdened with emotional fatigue, recognizing the need to rejuvenate to better engage with your clients. Your initial step may be to get some rest, schedule a day dedicated to self-care, or step away from your professional duties for a brief break.

Professionals often ask me: "I've taken a self-care break and got plenty of rest; why don't I feel rejuvenated?"

In the thick of the pandemic, as I poured my energy into supporting others through my private practice and classes, I reached my crisis point. The weight of collective anxiety and personal responsibility became overwhelming. Seeking relief, I paused to reset, immersing myself in the familiar self-care rituals. I rested, took meditative walks, and deepened my Reiki and meditation practices. These efforts brought physical relief and inner peace, yet something within remained unfulfilled—an emptiness that physical rest and mental relaxation could not touch.

In this quiet acknowledgment of my inner void, I turned inward, seeking guidance from my Soul. I engaged in *Soul Journaling*, a process of asking a question followed by free writing to tap into the wisdom that lay beneath the surface. The message from my Soul was unmistakable: It longed not for simple relaxation and stillness but for a space where intentional movement and music could flow freely. Since then, my daily practice has been enriched by intentional movement and music that touches my Soul deeply. The rhythm and melodies became a language through which my Soul could speak and heal.

> *As we peel back the layers of routine self-care, we often uncover spaces within us that remain unfilled, untouched by the typical wellness routines.*

Self-care and Soul-care are concepts that often overlap but stem from different approaches to well-being.

> *Self-care refers to the practices and activities we engage in regularly to reduce stress and maintain and enhance our short- and long-term health and well-being.*

Self-care is about caring for the physical body, mental health, and emotional needs. It's the kind of care that helps us stay functional and balanced in our day-to-day lives. Examples of self-care include getting enough sleep, eating healthy foods, exercising, managing stress, and taking time for relaxing activities.

> *Soul-care delves into the core of one's being, embracing activities and practices that resonate with our deepest values, beliefs, and sense of purpose, fostering a profound connection with our authentic self.*

It's about nourishing the Soul, attending to spiritual needs, and ensuring emotional and existential fulfillment.

While self-care tends to be more practical and physical, Soul-care is more abstract and spiritual. However, both are crucial for a holistic approach to health. They support each other and are often integrated; for example, yoga can be considered both self-care (physical exercise) and Soul-care (spiritual practice).

As we progress through this chapter, I'll present a range of Soul-care practices designed to align with your individuality, taste, and specific needs. In the meantime, open yourself to the understanding that Soul-care delves deeper than standard self-care, offering a unique pathway to enrichment.

> *Self-care keeps us well-functioning, while Soul-care makes our lives deeply meaningful.*

Thomas Moore beautifully articulates the journey of Soulful Living. His seminal book *Care of the Soul: A Guide for Cultivating Depth and Sacredness in Everyday Life* invites readers to see the extraordinary within the ordinary. He emphasizes that every aspect of day-to-day life can be filled with soulfulness, transforming the mundane into something sacred.

Our sacred responsibility as professionals is to care for our Souls in our daily lives. This way, we can be fully present and caring in our work, looking after our body, Soul, and spirit. When we listen to our inner voice, we can do our jobs better and help our clients. Then, we can also help them connect with their Soul and listen to their inner voice to guide them in their lives.

How can we allow our inner voice to shape our journey and guide us toward deeper understanding and personal evolution?

> *Initiating the profound journey of engaging with our internal guidance system involves embracing soulfulness in our lives and caring for our Soul, then posing questions and attentively listening to the insights it offers.*

Begin the Conversation: Ask Within

Engaging with our Souls and asking meaningful questions opens us to intuitive guidance and insights that foster personal growth. Once comfortable with this inner dialogue, you can encourage your clients to embark on a similar path.

Our Soul, the essence of our being, craves growth and fulfillment. It's not just survival, achievements, or productivity that nourish our Soul, but *the richness of life's experiences.*

Our Souls yearn for learning, potential, and alignment with our higher purpose.

Therefore, our questions should resonate on a higher plane than mundane concerns. Instead of asking, "What do I want?" or "What should I do?", we ask:

- ᴥ What does my Soul want to tell me today?
- ᴥ What wisdom do you have for me today?
- ᴥ What am I meant to learn here?

  ↪ What is this (pain, fear, etc.) here to teach me?

  ↪ What is the higher lesson in this situation?

  ↪ What is my spiritual lesson in this situation?

Remember a few fundamental principles when seeking guidance from your Soul. Begin by centering and grounding yourself. After posing your questions, be patient and let your Soul speak.

> *Approach your Soul with openness and without urgent expectations. Let the questions unfold naturally. Engage all your senses. Don't just listen—watch and feel. Release the need for immediate answers and trust that they will come when the time is right.*

The Unfolding Dialogue: Listening to Inner Guidance

Let's unpack what we mean when we say "inner guidance":

- Wisdom lives in the Soul.
- Deepening your Soul connectivity paves the way to a more profound relationship with your Divine Self.
- Your *Inner Wisdom* is the voice of the Soul, while the *Collective Wisdom* echoes the knowledge of the divine.
- *Intuition*, the language of your inner guidance, is the harmonious conductor of this internal symphony. This silent whisper unites the layers of our inner guidance and speaks to our Human Self.

Your intuition often uses signs, symbols, or patterns in your environment to get your attention, and it speaks through dreams, especially recurring ones.

To develop your understanding and reception of inner guidance, maintain a journal to capture recurring thoughts and insights. Note persistent elements—whether they manifest as dreams, numbers, words, colors, or physical sensations like goosebumps or an expansive heart feeling. Also, stay alert to phrases or concepts that repeatedly appear in songs, books, or conversations; these are how your Soul converses with you, widening the pathways for its voice to reach you.

How do you recognize an answer from your Soul? It might:

- ∿ Provide a sense of freshness
- ∿ Catch you by surprise
- ∿ Initially, feel odd, only to reveal its relevance later
- ∿ Introduce unexpected phrases or terms
- ∿ Evoke an expansive, freeing sensation rather than one of constriction

Engaging with your Soul by asking questions and listening attentively means you are tuning into your Inner Wisdom. This wisdom is an authentic echo from the depths of your being, offering spontaneous, resonant responses that require no analysis—only *recognition and understanding.*

To put it plainly:

> *Inner Wisdom: This is your Soul's direct communication deep from within. The unfiltered truth resonates at the Soul level, not derived from learned information or rational deliberation.*
>
> *Intuition: This is the awareness and vehicle for Inner Wisdom, an instinctive knowing that surfaces effortlessly. It is the silent voice that needs no words yet speaks volumes.*

Many times in my life, I've experienced moments of sudden intuition that seemed to come from the depths of my Soul. These insights, which often didn't make sense at first, would later reveal a deeper wisdom that my Soul had grasped long before my conscious mind understood.

When we lived in New York, my husband and I would travel to Atlanta every couple of months, where I had the joy of teaching my dedicated community. In March 2020, right after several days filled with workshops, private sessions, and classes, I led a Reiki class on a Sunday. It was the day before our return trip. As I taught, I felt a profound sense of knowing deep inside that this particular Sunday class would stand out as significant in my memory, even though I couldn't pinpoint why I felt that way.

While demonstrating a Reiki session with a volunteer, an unexpected urge struck me—I took out my phone and asked a student to record the process. This impulse was mysterious; I simply acted on a whisper from within. The next morning at the airport, we noticed more people wearing masks. By the time we returned to New York, the city had begun its lockdown. Unknown to me then, that Reiki class would be the last I'd teach in person for the next three years as all our sessions moved online. Yet, somewhere deep down, my Soul seemed to have anticipated this shift, prompting me to capture that moment on video—a clip that would become a staple in our virtual classes for years to follow.

Three years on, returning to Atlanta to teach felt different. As we drove through the city, the first visit since the pandemic began, I noticed its transformation. New eateries, quaint food markets, picturesque parks with trails, and vibrant nightlife districts had sprung up, adding to Atlanta's charm. During this trip, an unexpected thought bubbled up within me—what if we moved back to Atlanta? The idea took hold, filling me with a sense of completeness I hadn't felt in years.

Bringing up the idea of leaving New York for Atlanta to my husband seemed daunting; there had been no sign he was contemplating such a change. Yet when I mustered the courage to share my thought, it turned out our visions were in sync. Just four months later, we found ourselves in a spacious corner apartment in a beautiful Atlanta building boasting floor-to-ceiling windows and a stunning view. Writing this book in our Atlanta apartment, embraced by privacy, comfort, and inspiring panoramas, was a gift to my Soul—a contrast to the confines of our New York living space.

Reflecting on these personal experiences, you may wonder if you've ever felt a similar stir within your own life. Have you encountered moments where a sudden, unexplained insight seemed to guide your decisions? Instances where your Soul seemed to speak directly to you, providing guidance that later proved to be profoundly insightful?

As we transition from my stories to your journey, consider the times when you've felt an inner nudge steering you toward a choice or action. These are the whispers of your Soul—echoes of an Inner Wisdom that often knows more than we consciously realize.

When you actively engage with these soulful exchanges in your day-to-day life, you tap into a source of insights that can profoundly enrich your personal journey and professional endeavors. This isn't about academic knowledge; it's a deeper, more instinctual understanding that arises from the core of your being.

When you seek guidance from your Soul and receive a response that resonates on a profound, immediate level, you are experiencing Inner Wisdom expressed through intuition. This intuitive understanding is instinctual, born from a place of deep inner connection, not from intellectual reasoning.

> *By integrating soulful dialogues into your everyday life, you naturally begin to access insights from your Soul, enriching both your personal path and professional practice with the profound depth and clarity that springs from Inner Wisdom.*

Why Connecting with the Soul is Empowering for You as a Professional

Your Soul communicates through the nuanced language of intuition, allowing for a more profound empathy and understanding of those in your care. Integrating guidance from your Soul and allowing your intuition to steer you broadens your perspective. For the Soulful Healer, nurturing a connection with one's Soul is not just a practice but a necessity.

Through your journey to becoming soulful, you tune in not only to what your clients articulate but also to the silent messages they express. This expanded awareness enriches your professional insight, granting you the ability to look beyond surface symptoms and address the deeper roots of their challenges.

> *The insight you receive through the connection with your Soul empowers you to trust in your capacity to discern the unspoken needs of your clients. It is this trust that fills you with the confidence to lead, to soothe, and to inspire.*

Moreover, your well-nourished Soul becomes a beacon, an example that encourages clients to seek that same level of soulful satisfaction in their lives.

By prioritizing the health of your Soul, you not only enrich your personal well-being but also enhance your professional practice. You become a testament to the transformative power of Soulful Living, an embodiment of the healing you facilitate.

Dedication to this soulful dialogue reveals that your Soul's wisdom doesn't just whisper in moments of solitude; it begins to speak with gentle authority even in the middle of a client session. This guidance becomes a lamp in the therapeutic encounter, illuminating hidden paths that may lead to breakthroughs. It informs your intuition, allowing you to perceive beneath the layers of spoken word and surface emotion, tapping into a deeper layer of healing.

> *Incorporating soulful practices into your professional routine cultivates an inner clarity that supports the therapeutic path. You become skillful at interpreting its language in real time, offering insights and interventions that are intuitively aligned with your client's most profound healing journey. This practice turns each session into a union of two Souls in dialogue, transcending the mechanics of technique and embracing the artistry of healing.*

Attributed to the 13th-century Persian poet Rumi: "The Soul has been given its own ears to hear things the mind does not understand."

Soulful Snapshot

Reflect on the transformative revelation experienced by my client, Mary, a somatic therapist and mother of four. In the middle of the identity shift of becoming an empty nester, Mary felt disoriented, expressing, "I lost myself in the journey of motherhood."

During a session where we embarked on the Journey into the Soul—a pivotal part of my healing practice—I felt an intuitive nudge from my Soul to guide her toward a profound connection with her late grandmother. With eyes closed, Mary envisioned a heartfelt dialogue with her beloved grandmother, seeking her wisdom. In this soulful exchange, she received a powerful reassurance: She had not lost herself but was ready to transmute her motherhood experiences into wisdom for the present moment.

As Mary emerged from this meditation, she said it felt like a switch got flipped, and she reconnected with her Soul and the essence of who she is.

This soulful awakening encouraged her sense of self and enhanced her professional practice. She learned to guide disassociating clients to seek guidance from their Souls, facilitating deeper healing. "One of the most empowering outcomes of this journey," she said, "has been overcoming imposter syndrome. I've realized my worth and feel more confident in my abilities. I'm more aligned with my Soul and my core values, who I am, and my true self. This newfound confidence has propelled me to work on my website and messaging, allowing me to be more visible and authentic in my interactions with the world."

As Mary continued her practice, she maintained a daily dialogue with her Soul. Over the next few months, she observed a profound shift: *Her clients began echoing this inner attunement,* increasingly seeking and embracing their inner guidance. Reflecting on her deepened Soul connection marked a transformative phase in her therapeutic approach.

This dual deepening of soulful engagement—within herself and with her clients—empowered Mary to foster profound and lasting healing, demonstrating the vital role of Soul-work in professional development and therapeutic success.

Mary's story is a testament to the transformative power of soulful practice. It illustrates that every professional can tap into a wellspring of Inner Wisdom when they embrace this journey.

> *As a professional dedicated to guiding others through the labyrinth of their troubles, tapping into your own Soul's wisdom offers an invaluable compass. Tuning into your Soul's subtle guidance, you shift from your functional role to embody a source of profound wisdom, empowering your clients to do the same.*

Soulful Exercise: Crafting Your Wheel of Soulful Living

To bring the entire presence of your Soul into your professional sessions, it's vital to start by cultivating soulfulness in every aspect of your life. Nurturing your Soul is not just a personal luxury; it's a professional necessity that enables you to connect deeply with clients. Through years of insightful conversations with my clients and students and from my journey, I've refined a list of essential *Soul-care practices*. These practices are designed for anyone seeking to nourish their Soul and ensure it resonates through their life.

1. Take a moment to review the 14 Soul-care practices below.

2. Reflect on which of the practices resonate with you the most and have the potential to bring more soulfulness into your life.

3. Choose eight practices you would like to focus on and include in your personal Wheel of Soulful Living.

4. Write down each chosen practice in one of the eight slices of the wheel.

5. As you write down each practice, feel free to modify or adapt the wording to make it more personal and meaningful to you or to add new practices.

6. Are you feeling creative? Get your colored pencils or markers and add a visual to each slice.

7. Once you have filled in all eight slices, take a moment to review your personalized wheel and visualize how incorporating these practices can enhance your Soulful Living.

8. Keep your wheel in a place where you can see it regularly as a reminder of the actions and intentions you have set for yourself.

9. Revisit and refresh. Return to this exercise every few months to realign your Wheel of Soulful Living with your current life circumstances. Update your chosen practices to reflect your evolving needs and aspirations, ensuring your path to soulfulness remains dynamic and responsive to your journey.

Fourteen Soul-Care Practices: Nurturing Your Deepest Self

1. *Contemplative Nature Walks:* Walking in nature to connect deeply with the earth and its rhythms, often in silence, to cultivate a sense of oneness with the natural world.

2. *Sacred Ritual Creation:* Designing personal rituals to honor transitions, celebrate achievements, or acknowledge losses, giving profound experiences a spiritual dimension.

3. *Creating a Personal Altar:* Designing a sacred space in your home as a focal point for spiritual practice. This altar can hold significant symbols, artifacts, images, crystals, candles, or natural elements that resonate with your spiritual journey as a daily reminder of your values and beliefs.

4. *Soulful Journaling:* Writing to explore the depths of your inner life, feelings, and Soul's desires, often through prompts that encourage introspection and self-discovery.

5. *Artistic Expression as Devotion:* Creating art as a form of spiritual practice, whether painting, music, writing, or dance, to express and connect with the divine or the essence of life.

6. *Mindfulness:* Mindful meditation, mindful cooking, mindful eating, and other expressions of mindful living; practicing presence and awareness to connect to the present moment on a profound level and touch a sense of unity with all.

7. *Spiritual Fellowship:* Gathering with others in sisterhoods and communities for shared spiritual growth, support, and communal practices.

8. *Silent Retreats:* Spending time in silence and solitude to listen to the voice of your inner being, often in a retreat setting that supports deep spiritual work.

9. *Guided Imagery and Visualization:* Using the imagination to visit inner landscapes, meet with aspects of the self, or connect with spiritual guides for insight and healing.

10. *Energy Work:* Engaging in practices such as Reiki, yoga, qigong, or tai chi, that work with the body's energy systems to enhance spiritual alignment and balance.

11. *Connecting with the Divine Feminine:* Engaging with practices that honor and invoke the energy of the Divine Feminine, such as working with goddess archetypes; embracing qualities like intuition, receptivity, and nurturing; or participating in women's circles and rituals that celebrate feminine wisdom and strength.

12. *Soul-Enriching Activities:* Embracing additional practices that nourish your Soul, such as traveling the world, tending a garden, indulging in daydreams, or any other activity that brings joy and fulfillment to your being.

13. *Intuitive Movement—Dance, Stretch, and Flow:* Moving in ways that feel instinctual and freeing, allowing you to connect deeply with your body's wisdom and the rhythm of your Soul.

14. *Aromatic Harmony:* Infusing your daily life with the comfort of essential oils and fragrances, which can calm, energize, and harmonize—engaging the senses to support soulful well-being.

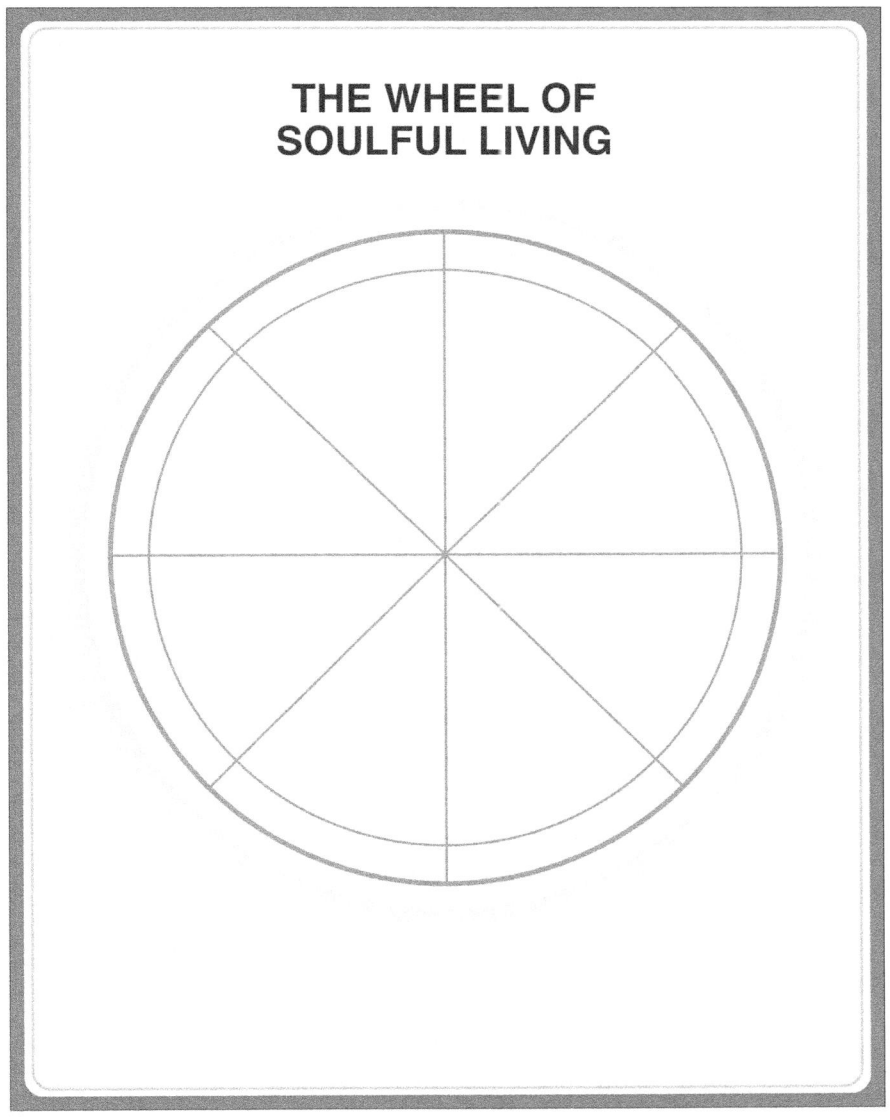

THE WHEEL OF SOULFUL LIVING

Once you've completed your Wheel of Soulful Living, you've begun a journey of reflection, identifying practices that resonate with your deepest self. Allow the insights from this creative process to settle within you as we shift our attention inward further.

As we turn the page from understanding to experience, let's now engage directly with the Soul. Join me in this guided visualization: Reconnect with Your Soul to converse with and embrace the wisdom within.

Guided Visualization: Reconnect with Your Soul

Let's take the connection with your Soul to a deeper level, engaging not just the mind but the spirit through the power of visualization.

When you are ready to begin the journey, find a comfortable position, take a deep breath, and listen to the audio you've downloaded, which is transcribed below.

Close your eyes, take a deep breath, then slowly exhale, allowing any tension to melt away.

Shift your focus to the middle of your forehead, to the place often referred to as the third eye. This is the window to your inner vision, the lens that can look inward to your deepest self.

Now, direct this inner gaze toward your heart area. Search for a small flame there. This may be hidden or just a mere spark, but know it is waiting to be found. Trust that it is there, the eternal flame of your Soul.

With your next breath, imagine this flame growing slightly brighter, fed by the oxygen of your breath, the commitment of your attention. Continue to breathe; with each inhale, see the flame becoming larger; with each exhale, see it shining brighter. Feel its warmth spread throughout your body. This light is the essence of your Soul, a symbol of your innate purity and wisdom.

As this light fills you, begin to engage in a dialogue with your Soul. Start by expressing your gratitude. Thank her for pouring her light into you in times of darkness. Thank her for the wisdom that guides you, the inspiration that uplifts you, and the love that surrounds you. Thank her for the strength she gives you to face challenges and the peace she offers in moments of quiet.

Now, gently ask your Soul what she needs. Be still and listen; feel her response within your body. It might come as an emotion, a physical sensation, or a whisper of thought. Visualize yourself gently and softly, providing her with these needs.

Notice how you feel when you are in tune with your Soul. There might be a sense of completeness, a feeling of peace, or an upwelling of love. Acknowledge these feelings; they are signs of your deepening connection. If any sadness or difficult emotions arise, make space for them too. Offer them compassion and sit with them gently, as they are part of your journey and your conversation with your Soul.

As you prepare to wrap up the conversation with your Soul, commit yourself—promise to continue this dialogue, regularly check in with your Soul, and nurture this relationship.

When you're ready, take a few more deep, intentional breaths. With each breath, become more aware of the physical space around you. Wiggle your fingers and toes, gently move your head from side to side, and open your eyes when you feel ready, returning to the present moment carrying the wisdom of your Soul with you.

Reflect on the Chapter: Questions to Consider

1. What are the moments in your life when you felt the most authentic connection with your Soul?

2. What practices from your Wheel of Soulful Living have you found most effective in reconnecting with your Soul? Why do you think they resonated with you?

3. How can the insights from the "Reconnecting with Your Soul" visualization guide your future Soul-care practices?

4. How can you integrate your Soul's nurturing into your daily professional life to serve others better?

5. What commitment can you make to ensure regular dialogue with your Soul, and how will you honor this commitment?

From Words to Action: Applying This Chapter's Lessons

Moving from the insights of this chapter into tangible steps in our daily lives is critical to nurturing a genuine connection with your Soul. This chapter has provided the tools and understanding to recognize the Soul's language and craft a Wheel of Soulful Living that resonates with your deepest self. It's about turning inward, acknowledging your Soul's voice, and taking the time to listen and respond.

Incorporating Soul-care practices into your routine is more than self-improvement; it's a sacred act of reclaiming your true self. Whether through contemplative walks, creating personal altars, or engaging in mindful meditation, each practice is a step toward a more authentic existence. Engage with these practices regularly and let them be a compass that guides you back to your Soul, especially during times of disconnect or distress.

To seamlessly integrate this soulful approach into your professional work, set aside a few moments before each session to center yourself and connect with your Soul. This practice will help you enter a state of heightened intuition and presence, allowing you to be more attuned to your client's needs. During sessions, maintain an open channel to your Soul's guidance, trusting the subtle nudges and insights that arise. Encourage clients to engage in similar practices, guiding them to explore their inner landscapes for healing and insight.

Let the lessons of this chapter be a living dialogue between you and your Soul, a dialogue that evolves as you do. Embrace this ongoing conversation, and watch as your life transforms, reflecting the soulful authenticity you cultivate each day.

> *Authenticity isn't a destination but a journey of constant alignment with your inner truth.*

Unfolding the Next Layer

As we draw this chapter to a close, we reflect on the profound journey of nurturing an authentic connection with our Soul. By engaging with the Wheel of Soulful Living, you have begun to incorporate Soul-care practices seamlessly into the rhythm of your daily life. Crafting your wheel, choosing practices that resonate with your essence, and integrating them into your routine is more than self-care—it's a ritualistic embrace of your core being.

The Wheel of Soulful Living is a personal tool and a professional compass, guiding you to navigate sessions with intuition and empathy. Through this, you may find that the insights collected from your Soul enrich your practice, bringing a depth to your sessions that resonates with the authentic journey of both healer and client. Mika's and Mary's stories of healing and empowerment are just two examples of the potential in this sacred professional path, highlighting how Soul-work can illuminate the therapeutic process for profound and lasting impact.

As you venture into the next chapter, carry forward the curiosity ignited here. The practices and reflections you've embraced serve as a foundation for the deeper exploration that lies ahead.

> *The insight you gain by listening to the whispers of your Soul is the first step toward accessing a broader wisdom— the collective symphony of shared human experiences and ancestral knowledge.*

Chapter 4

KEY # 4—INSIGHT
Tapping into Inner and Collective Wisdom

Before You Begin, Download These Resources:

"The Sanctuary of Your Dreams" guided visualization audio and the "Oracle Cards Reflection" form in color.

https://beaconout.com/bsr

As dawn stretched its golden fingers over the horizon, an elder of the tribe sat with a circle of children, the new day's light washing over their attentive faces. "Listen well," he began, his voice as steady as the ancient rocks surrounding them, "for I will tell you of the two wolves."

"Inside every person," the elder said, "there are two wolves locked in a constant battle. One wolf is full of anger, jealousy, sorrow, regret, greed, arrogance, self-pity, guilt, resentment, inferiority, lies, false pride, superiority, and ego." He paused, his gaze meeting each pair of young eyes. "This wolf is dark as the stormy sky and as restless as the wind."

"The other wolf," he continued, his voice softening, "is full of joy, peace, love, hope, serenity, humility, kindness, benevolence, empathy, generosity, truth, compassion, and faith. This wolf is light as the first snow and as tranquil as the still waters."

The children, absorbed in the story, leaned in as the elder spoke: "These wolves are in a fierce battle for control over our spirits."

A small hand went up; a young voice asked, "Which wolf will win?"

The elder looked at the child and said warmly, "The one you feed."

He leaned back and added, "But remember, it is not only a choice between anger and joy, darkness and light. *It is a choice that speaks of balance. Even the dark wolf has its place—teaching us the cost of giving in to fear and isolation, reminding us that strength without compassion is hollow.* In feeding the good wolf, we acknowledge the lessons of the other. *We do not fight or ignore the dark wolf*; instead, we acknowledge and learn from it, for to deny one is to live without the full wisdom of both."

Throughout the years, as I've heard various versions of this Native American folktale, often attributed to the Cherokee, a question has lingered in my mind. What if the so-called "good" wolf embodies qualities like joy and peace and a profound alignment with its Inner Wisdom, an intuitive, deep-seated knowing that offers guidance? In contrast, the "bad" wolf, characterized by darker emotions, may be seen as disconnected from these inner qualities, its actions driven by external forces and immediate reactions rather than an understanding that comes from within. This interpretation suggests that our journey toward wisdom involves a conscious choice to tune in to our internal compass and values, feeding the parts of ourselves that are anchored in a deeper sense of knowing and purpose.

In ancient times, life was simpler and less busy. Without modern technology, social media, and our fast-paced world, people could be more present and mindful in their daily lives.

This increased presence enabled people to be more in tune with the wisdom surrounding them. They could better listen to their intuition, observe the natural world, and learn from the experiences and knowledge passed down through generations.

This deep-rooted connection to wisdom guided them in making decisions, solving problems, and living harmoniously with nature and one another.

> *Today, we can reconnect with this ancient wisdom by silencing the noise and distractions that cloud our minds. By listening to our intuition and honoring its guidance, we can tap into the unlimited source of wisdom within us and the universe.*

In Western society, there is a strong emphasis on relying primarily on our intellectual capabilities. This approach often encourages individuals to focus solely on mental intelligence, neglecting other forms of intelligence that contribute to a more holistic understanding of the world. *By limiting ourselves to mental intelligence alone, we unintentionally restrict our capacity to connect with our Inner Wisdom, which can be accessed by integrating emotional, intuitive, and somatic intelligence alongside our intellect.*

Wisdom's Symphony: Orchestrating Inner Insight with Collective Consciousness

> " *Each of us possesses a natural Inner Wisdom, a guiding voice that is as constant as the beating of our hearts. It is a timeless navigator, whispering insights collected not from books or lectures but from the very essence of our being. When we dare to listen, we truly unlock a tank of knowledge and understanding that can enrich our lives in immeasurable ways.* "

This wisdom is not loud or demanding; it does not demand attention within the cacophony of daily life. Instead, it requires us to seek silence, be still, and listen. In this stillness, we can truly hear the subtle yet profound guidance that our Inner Wisdom offers. It is there within each of us, patiently waiting for us to pause, listen, and follow its direction.

Picture your Inner Wisdom as a treasure chest filled with life experiences, knowledge, and intuition, all mixed to create a brilliant map of understanding. This invaluable guide helps us navigate life's challenges, make better choices, and grow from triumphs and setbacks.

Wisdom extends beyond the individual. Carl Jung introduced the concept of the *collective unconscious,* which encompasses shared human knowledge and experiences. I interpret this as a *Collective Wisdom* we can all access.

Jung, a distinguished Swiss psychiatrist and psychoanalyst, expanded upon the foundational work of his mentor, Sigmund Freud, by exploring the depths of the human psyche. Jung's profound insights led him to theorize the existence of a collective unconscious, setting a transformative tone in the understanding of human wisdom.

Unlike the individualized wisdom cultivated through personal experiences, Jung imagined a more universal dimension of wisdom. He believed this collective layer of the unconscious is a source of profound wisdom, encompassing universal themes and patterns that emerge in myths, dreams, and narratives across human societies.

These archetypal images and stories are not developed individually but are innate to the human psyche, deeply influencing personal insight and cultural expressions. Through engaging with these shared symbols and narratives, individuals can tap into the Collective Wisdom that transcends personal experience.

> *We live in a pool of wisdom, an endless tank of insight waiting to be embraced.*

Jung's Dream:
Exploring the Ocean of Consciousness

In the vivid dream of Carl Jung, as described in his autobiography, he navigates a house of many layers, each descending into a more profound historical period. He begins in a salon decorated with Rococo elegance and valuable paintings, suggestive of a cultivated conscious mind. Compelled to explore further, Jung moves downward to the house's older levels, which reflect the personal unconscious with medieval elements and darker corners.

Venturing into the cellar, he uncovers Roman brickwork, symbolizing the ancient aspects of the psyche. Finally, he reaches a primal, dust-covered cave, finding traces of early human life, including skulls.

These deepest layers represent the collective unconscious, a kingdom of universal memories and experiences shared among all humans. Jung's descent through the house is a metaphor for the journey inward toward the core of the psyche, where personal and Collective Wisdom lives in silent testimony to our shared humanity.

My interpretation of Jung's dream aligns with the belief that personal growth and enlightenment are accessible through introspection and connecting with the collective tank of human experience. By delving into and embracing the lessons our collective unconscious offers, we empower ourselves with a broader, more profound compass of understanding, fostering personal transformation and healing.

Jung's Theory in Practice

Carl Jung's dream offers a profound metaphor for the depths of the human psyche, unpacking the layers of consciousness that expand from the individual to the collective.

As professionals seeking to facilitate deep healing and meaningful growth, we can draw upon Jung's insights to guide our clients on their inner journeys. Just as Jung navigated through the symbolic rooms and layers of his psyche, we, too, can provide the means for ourselves and our clients to explore the various levels of consciousness. Here, in the hands-on application of Jung's theoretical landscape, we find a collection of tools and practices designed to unlock the wisdom within and form a connection with the collective narrative of humanity.

You can incorporate tools such as meditation, writing, keeping dream journals, or intuition diaries to capture the whispers of your subconscious mind.

Beyond meditation, dream journaling, and intuitive writing, consider integrating practices such as mindfulness to heighten awareness and thoughtful reading of philosophical texts for deeper insight. Working with pendulums can help connect with the subconscious. Immersing in nature and embracing traditional cultural practices can link to ancestral wisdom. Engage in therapeutic techniques, artistic expression, and bodywork practices such as Reiki, yoga, qigong, or tai chi to synchronize body and mind, revealing pathways to deeper wisdom. Group dialogues and ceremonial practices can also unearth collective insights.

Among the wealth of tools available for accessing wisdom, I'd like to share two that I have used for many years with great success: guided visualizations and oracle cards.

Guided Visualization as a Tool
for Inner Discovery

> *Guided visualizations are structured exercises that lead individuals through a series of mental images and scenarios, tapping into the subconscious to reveal inner truths and connect with the universal narratives found in our Collective Wisdom. They create a safe, imaginative space for exploration and discovery, encouraging the mind to open to intuition and deeper understanding.*

Through the art of visualization, we tap into this deep-rooted power and envision images that resonate with our deepest selves.

Norman Doidge, a psychiatrist and author renowned for his books on brain science, explores neuroplasticity and investigates this concept, showing how the brain can transform and heal in response to thought patterns and imagery.

Antonio Damasio, a distinguished neuroscientist and professor, complements this understanding by revealing the integral role emotions play in shaping our decisions and experiences. These mental concepts are not mere fantasies but are tools that, when used with intention and guidance, can foster tangible changes in our psychological and emotional states.

As a professional, you can craft guided visualizations tailored to your client's needs or use established ones that resonate with your work. When creating a visualization, consider the objective—to calm, inspire, or uncover hidden thoughts. Start with a relaxing scenario, use descriptive language to engage the senses, and gently guide the client toward the insight you aim to uncover. Remember, the journey should be as meaningful as the destination.

You're also welcome to use the guided visualization scripts provided in each chapter of this book (and remember that you have access to the audio versions of these visualizations as well). They are designed to facilitate a connection with Inner and Collective Wisdom, aiding your clients on their path to self-awareness and personal growth.

People frequently ask how I developed the skill to create guided visualizations instead of relying on pre-written scripts. The ability to create guided visualizations on the spot wasn't inherent to me; it's a skill I've honed over the years.

After attending the Hoffman Quadrinity Process® in 2003, I gained the courage to create tailored guided visualizations for my clients. Founded by Bob Hoffman in 1967, this week-long residential retreat helped me identify and break away from negative behaviors, automatic tendencies, and thought patterns rooted in my childhood.

While attending this personal growth retreat, I connected with my inner child, the inner children of my parents, as well as my spirit and Soul. This profound connection was facilitated through a series of brilliant exercises, including guided visualizations. This life-changing experience inspired me to use guided visualization more in my work, and I have become a strong advocate of this valuable tool.

Drawing from my transformative experiences and the insights gained from esteemed thinkers in the field, it becomes evident to me that:

> *The human mind possesses a remarkable healing ability rooted in the power of imagery and imagination.*

Here are some guidelines you can follow when creating guided visualizations for your clients:

1. *Clarify the Purpose:* Define the goal of the visualization. What change or realization do you hope to bring about in the client? Consider therapeutic goals such as relaxation, insight, emotional release, or connecting with Inner Wisdom.

2. *Craft a Welcoming Beginning:* Start with a relaxation technique to calm the mind and body. Deep breathing, progressive muscle relaxation, or a peaceful setting can help the client become receptive to the visualization.

3. *Engage the Senses:* Use descriptive language to create a vivid scenario. Include details that engage all the senses—sight, sound, touch, taste, and smell—to make the experience immersive.

4. *Guide Gradually:* Transition smoothly from one scene to the next. Ensure each step is connected and leads the client deeper into the visualization without abrupt changes that might disrupt the flow.

5. *Encourage Emotional Connection:* Include elements that resonate emotionally with the client. This could involve revisiting positive memories, imagining achieving future goals, or connecting with a sense of peace.

6. *Invite Exploration:* Pose open-ended questions or scenarios that encourage self-reflection and exploration.

7. *Ensure a Safe Return:* Conclude the visualization by gently guiding clients back to their present surroundings. Reorient them to the here and now, ensuring they feel grounded before ending the session.

8. *Personalize:* Adapt the visualization to the individual needs of the client. The more personalized it is, the more effective it will be.

Another favorite tool that serves as a mirror to the subconscious is *oracle cards*, which resonate deeply with Carl Jung's insights into the collective unconscious. These cards, rich with symbols and archetypes, provide a tangible means for both you and your clients to engage with the profound messages of our shared human experience. Integrating oracle cards into your practice invites an exploration of these universal themes, facilitating personal growth and transformative insights.

Oracle Cards as a Gateway to Inner Wisdom

" *Oracle cards are a unique and powerful tool for those seeking insight from your Inner Wisdom and the Collective Wisdom. Each deck, unique in its thematic and artistic expression, is a collection of symbols and imagery intended to resonate with the user intuitively. Unlike the structured tradition of tarot, oracle cards offer a more fluid and personalized approach to self-reflection and discovery.* "

When you use an oracle card and begin by looking at the pictures, you are engaging your *conscious mind* as you are actively looking at and thinking about what you see.

As you start to reflect on the images and associate them with personal memories or feelings, you are tapping into the *subconscious mind*. The subconscious is stored and can be recalled without deliberate effort.

If deeper, spontaneously arising memories or profound insights come to the surface, ones that you were not initially aware of or that feel revelatory, you could be accessing the *unconscious mind*. The unconscious mind holds deeper, often repressed or unrecognized feelings and memories.

" *When we pick an oracle card after asking a question, the cards become a reflective surface for our deepest thoughts and feelings. We don't expect a direct answer from the card. The card is more like a reminder of a thought or feeling inside us that we might not have paid attention to before. It helps us to listen to our own inner voice, which we've been tuning out.* "

Whether seeking guidance for the day or clarity on a specific question, start your interaction with the cards with intention. Create a sacred and reflective space, followed by grounding yourself in the present moment.

As you shuffle the deck with your question in mind, the act becomes meditative, aligning your energy with the cards. Selecting a card is an exercise in trusting your intuition and understanding that the card drawn is what is needed at that moment. It's not just the imagery that is important, but the emotions and thoughts that surface as you reflect on the card's deeper meanings.

Through observation, reflection, and journaling, oracle cards offer fresh perspectives and invite a deeper understanding of oneself and one's circumstances. They encourage an *active dialogue with the self*, sparking insights that may have remained unearthed without this meditative practice.

This personal and thoughtful journey with oracle cards is about seeking answers and embracing the questions that lead to self-awareness and personal growth. As we explore these cards, *we become both the seeker and the finder,* navigating the rich inner insight revealed through the cards.

I've outlined the steps for selecting a card and reflecting on its message later in this chapter as an exercise. You can use this process for yourself or with a client.

> *The power of oracle cards lies in their ability to serve as a conduit, linking conscious awareness with the subtle whispers of our subconscious mind, facilitating a journey of self-discovery, and empowering us to uncover the hidden wisdom within.*

My Love Story with One Specific Deck: The Women of Wisdom Cards

At the end of an appointment with my therapist many years ago, she asked if I wanted to anchor our session by choosing a card. "Sure," I said, curious about what would happen. I didn't know it then, but the deck she used would one day become a method I use to guide my clients.

The card I chose was a biblical woman standing in the middle of a storm like a pillar, with angel wings around her. My therapist read its message aloud, "Lot's Wife. Holding onto her past."

The story of Lot's wife, an ancient biblical woman, is told in Genesis 19. Angels urged Lot and his family to escape the upcoming destruction of their city. The command was given to run without looking behind. While escaping, Lot's wife turned to look back, and she was turned into a pillar of salt.

I heard the oracle card's message from within: "You possess the ability to choose. Will you continue holding onto your past or release it so you can move forward in life?"

I had resisted letting go of the old baggage I had carried from the past. Choosing this card revealed its impact on my life and helped me find the courage to let go of my resistance.

It wasn't just the message, the picture, or the story. It was a moment where everything clicked, all the awareness, the many conversations I had with my therapist, all of it. My Soul was speaking. And for the first time, I indeed heard.

I bought the cards the following day and have used them for myself and others ever since. In 2022, a decade after consistently using the Women of Wisdom cards in my signature healing experience, the Journey into the Soul sessions, I decided to write this book. At that time, the cards existed only in Hebrew, so I felt compelled to contact the creator, share their profound impact on my personal and professional life, and request her permission to include them in my book.

That phone call in July 2022 turned both of our lives around. Not only did we become friends—or perhaps soul-sisters—but Judith Jungman-Saadon, a psychologist and women's group facilitator, shared that she was translating the cards into English. She agreed to let me help her align the English wording with the language used in women's empowerment and spiritual communities in the US. I felt honored to provide input and support during the translation process. When I held the English version of the cards for the first time in 2023, I was filled with tears of joy and a sense of pride.

The Women of Wisdom cards possess an ancient wisdom that acts as a catalyst, enabling us to access profound insights from the Inner and Collective Wisdom. These cards bring to life the stories and the voice of the biblical women. Through the cards, we meet brave and wise women, beautiful and resourceful women who know their purpose, challenge their fate, and rebuild their lives.

The passage from Ronna J. Detrick's book *Rewriting Eve* resonates deeply with me. Detrick writes:

"Despite a long history of oppression, silencing, and shame, these women and their stories inexplicably persist. They are brave, wise, vulnerable, and gentle—just like us. They have known tremendous loss, fear, and pain—just like us They have been overlooked and underestimated—just like us. They have been misunderstood and dismissed—just like us. They have survived—just like us."

Drawing from my experience as a professional, I incorporate various card decks into my sessions and workshops. The Women of Wisdom cards are undoubtedly the most accurate, rich, and profound cards I have ever used.

Soulful Snapshot

The following story demonstrates the power of tapping into the Collective Wisdom through the Women of Wisdom cards.

Meet Mia. Confronting cancer when she was 14, followed by severe health challenges, forced her to be strong and show her family that she was a fighter. She grew up even more resilient, ready to confront any challenge with determination. As an adult, she worked as a crisis disaster manager, and even when cancer returned, she fought bravely and overcame it.

As a continuous caretaker and crisis solver, she unintentionally shut off parts of herself, becoming an overachiever who lived for others' dramas. Recognizing the toll these roles took was the first step toward healing. Addressing her traumas holistically has begun to free deep-seated beliefs and reawaken her Soul's more tender, spirited parts—her compassion, spontaneity, and elegance.

After a few months of therapeutic sessions, as Mia worked through her past trauma, she took the Journey into the Soul with me. At the end of the deep healing experience, I suggested she select a Women of Wisdom card. Without seeing the picture or message on the cards, she picked Yael, the biblical woman who embodied sensitivity and courage.

In the story from the Bible, Yael is known for her decisive act that ended the oppression of her people. When Sisera, the commander of the Canaanite army who had cruelly oppressed the Israelites for two decades, fled from a lost battle and sought refuge in Yael's tent, she welcomed him. She offered him comfort with milk and a place to rest, but as he lay sleeping, Yael seized the moment to stop the oppression. Her act of killing Sisera was one of courage, born out of deep compassion and care for her people who had suffered under his rule. Yael took this bold step, overcoming her fears, to liberate her people from Sisera's long-standing domination and cruelty.

Mia's takeaway from the story was that Yael encourages her to conquer her fears and find strength in her softness. This insight reinforced the therapeutic work we'd been doing, focused on healing past trauma and teaching Mia to feel safe enough to soften her heart. Yael's fusion of bravery with her gentle and tender qualities truly inspired Mia. Experiencing this unique balance, Mia felt empowered to let go of her former self and rediscover the softer, more compassionate aspects of herself that had been hidden.

When I checked with Mia two years after she took the Journey into the Soul, she said: "Thanks to the wisdom I received from Yael, fear has not been a choice in my life for a while now. I have noticed my softer side is very present now. I have been choosing to accept my feminine power. I am using it to patiently be on my journey, savoring being present with each step and making conscious choices to overcome any barriers I place on myself. I am living with intention and being loving and compassionate toward myself."

While I sincerely appreciate using the Women of Wisdom cards in my Journey into the Soul sessions, it's important to remember that other tools can also effectively access wisdom. Embracing various approaches allows us to find the best method for our unique spiritual journey.

Why Integrating Inner and Collective Wisdom Transforms Your Practice

Whether you are a professional, or an individual seeking guidance, you can profoundly enhance your practice by acknowledging the importance of drawing on Inner and Collective Wisdom.

> *Opening up to the Collective Wisdom strengthens collaborative problem-solving and creative ways to receive support and fosters empathy and compassion. Such an integrated approach equips us with the tools for significant growth and contributes to a more empathetic and interconnected world.*

Holistic methods that engage the entire being—mind, body, spirit, and soul—allow for comprehensive growth and healing. Enriching your sessions with meditation, oracle card insights, creative visualization, or other creative tools unlocks doors to Inner Wisdom, providing access to previously untapped areas of the psyche. These practices offer clients fresh perspectives and a deeper understanding of their situations.

Moreover, engaging with the Inner and Collective Wisdom enriches the approach to personal challenges, guiding clients to trust their internal compass. This deepens the practice and empowers clients, granting them a balanced perspective to face life's difficulties with newfound confidence and poise.

> " *Embracing the intuitive insights that live within the self, and the shared experiences that unite us, elevates your work beyond traditional methods, leading to more profound healing outcomes, and distinguishes you as a unique professional in your field.* "

Soulful Exercise:
Intuitive Oracle Journey and Reflection

Engage in a mindful exploration of self-awareness and intuition with the "Intuitive Oracle Journey." This step-by-step process is designed to deepen your connection with your Inner Wisdom through oracle cards. To enhance your experience and capture your insights, use the Oracle Cards Reflection Form to take notes as you progress through each stage of the journey.

Choose a deck of oracle cards that resonates with you and follow these steps:

1. *Create Your Sacred Space:* Design a serene space for your practice. Set a tranquil atmosphere by lighting a candle, burning incense, or playing calming music. Take a moment to breathe deeply and anchor yourself in the now.

2. *Clarify Your Intention:* Clearly articulate the purpose of your oracle card session. Are you seeking guidance, looking for insight, or needing affirmation? Write down your question or intention to solidify your focus.

3. *Connect with the Cards:* Concentrate on your intention as you shuffle the deck. Trust that your intuition will guide you to the card that now offers the message you need.

4. *Select with Intuition:* Draw a card from the deck when you feel compelled. Trust the spontaneous impulse that leads you to choose—this is your intuition speaking.

5. *Observe and Reflect:* Take a detailed look at your selected card. Notice the images, colors, and symbols, and be mindful of your initial emotional and mental responses. Observe the card without relating it to yourself, focusing on what you see. If there are

people shown, consider what is happening for them, the narrative suggested by the imagery, and their emotions.

6. *Journal Your Impressions:* Document your observations of the card. What narratives do the visuals on the card suggest? Write about the card and its elements as you see them, focusing on the story it tells rather than how it relates to you.

7. *Contemplate the Message:* Now, reflect on how the card's message relates to your intention. If the card could talk, what would it say? If the card could speak directly to your situation, what would it say? Allow your intuition to interpret the card's symbolism in the context of your question.

8. *Carry the Insights Forward:* Keep the card in a visible place or with you to remind you of its message. Be open to signs and synchro-nicities throughout your day that may relate to the card's wisdom.

9. *Reflect and Integrate:* Ponder the card's guidance over the next few days. How does its message weave into the fabric of your life? Note any shifts in perception or awareness that arise.

ORACLE CARD REFLECTION

My intention for this session

The question I am concentrating on

The card I selected

The imagery I observe on the card (images, colors, symbols)

The story that the imagery on the card expresses

My initial emotional response to the card

If this card could talk, what would it say?

How the card's message relates to aspects of my life

To embody the wisdom of this card, I will....

Transitioning from our dive into the depths of Collective Wisdom and inner insight, let us now journey inward through a guided visualization to uncover the hidden treasures within the layers of our unconscious.

Guided Visualization:
The Sanctuary of Your Dreams

This guided visualization is inspired by the profound dream journey of Carl Jung, taking us through the layered depths of the unconscious as detailed in his autobiography. As we embark on this meditative exploration, we connect with the collective cosmic library of human wisdom and experience, much like Jung's own descent into the historic levels of his psyche.

When you are ready to begin the journey, find a comfortable position, take a deep breath, and listen to the audio you've downloaded, which is transcribed below.

Close your eyes and take a few deep breaths, inhaling peace and exhaling any tension. With each breath, feel yourself become relaxed and centered.

Visualize yourself approaching a beautiful, tranquil home—your island of peace. As you enter, you start walking and exploring the beauty of the floor, ceiling, wall art, and furniture. You take in the harmonizing colors and the smells of the house.

Notice how all your worries and concerns are left behind. This house is a sanctuary of comfort and safety, feeling like home. As you walk through it, feel the space welcoming you with open arms, inviting you to explore the depth of your imagination.

You come upon a staircase that leads down to a cozy basement, a place where hidden treasures await discovery. A charming, old-fashioned metal handle set into the floor hints at a secret passage. Gently pulling it, you reveal a beautiful staircase. With each step down, you feel safer and more secure.

You reach the bottom to discover an ancient cave. The air is cool, and slivers of light shine through the cracks in the stone, providing just enough light to see by. The serene silence wraps around you like a comforting shawl. Continue walking until you arrive at an archway leading into an inner chamber.

You enter the room to find a tall, beautiful woman in a white dress waiting for you, a wise embodiment of knowledge. She moves with poise and grace and hands you a treasure box, inviting you to sit with her on a stone bench. "This is your Dreams Box," she says. "Inside, you'll find the essence of dreams past and the seeds of dreams to come. It will guide you to make them real."

You sit down and open the box. Observe its contents closely. Notice the drawings, words, and symbols that tell the stories of your dreams. The wise woman whispers, "You can bring your dreams to life," before she kisses your forehead, leaving you with the box.

Look inside the open box. Recognize the symbols, the sketches, and the words. Allow the stories of your dreams to unfold before you. Take your time to absorb this sacred information. What do you see? What could these symbols, drawings, and words suggest about your dreams? Explore and listen. Don't try to interpret their meaning. Wait, and allow their meaning to be revealed to you.

When you're ready, gently close the Dreams Box, and in your heart, thank the wise woman for her gift.

Carry the box with you as you climb the stairs back to the house, bringing the wisdom of the cave with you.

Feel the ground beneath you as you bring your awareness back to the present.

When you open your eyes, reflect on the experience for a few moments.

Write down or draw what came up for you—the symbols, the words, the feelings, and any insights about your dreams. Reflect on how these insights can guide you toward realizing your dreams in waking life.

To continue nurturing the seeds of insight planted during your visualization, consider creating a "Dreams Box." This can be a physical box where you collect items that symbolize the insights and aspirations that surfaced. It might include notes, sketches, or any small object that represents a piece of your vision. Periodically return to this box to add new items or reflect on the ones already there, allowing it to be a tangible reminder and motivator of the dreams your Soul is urging you to fulfill.

Reflect on the Chapter: Questions to Consider

1. Reflect on a recent challenge or conflict: which "wolf" did you feed in your response, and how did that choice affect the outcome and your inner peace?

2. In moments of decision, how can you better listen to your Inner Wisdom over external pressures?

3. What practices can you introduce to your routine to help quiet the mind and connect with Inner and Collective Wisdom?

4. How has technology impacted your ability to connect with your intuitive self, and what changes could you make to address this?

5. How can you better recognize and honor the wisdom from your internal guidance system?

From Words to Action: Applying This Chapter's Lessons

To integrate the insights from this chapter into your life, begin by dedicating time each day to silence and stillness. This could be through meditation, nature walks, or simply turning off digital devices for a period. Use this time to connect with and to cultivate mindfulness. Become aware of which "wolf" your actions are feeding; *notice when you're acting out of habit rather than intention.*

Keep a journal to document your dreams and intuitive experiences, noting any patterns or recurring symbols that may arise.

Add playfulness to your personal and professional life by experimenting using oracle cards and reflecting on the insight they bring.

Go through the guided visualization to help you connect with your dreams and then come up with ways to make them a reality. Keep dreaming!

Unfolding the Next Layer

For professionals who facilitate growth in others, embracing the teachings of the two wolves and tapping into Inner and Collective Wisdom is not merely personal; it expands the extent and depth of their work. This journey enhances a your ability to guide clients toward deeply intentional and insightfully informed choices.

By integrating a broad range of practices into your professional toolkit—including practices that aid in tapping into both Inner Wisdom and the Collective Wisdom—you can offer clients strategies to still their minds and connect with their internal guidance systems. This enriches the therapeutic experience by blending timeless wisdom with modern understanding.

This approach supports a shared exploration of the darker and lighter aspects within us all, providing a balanced and realistic approach to personal development and emotional healing.

The rewards of this reflective practice are immeasurable: It fosters personal growth, strengthens the therapeutic relationship, and cultivates a therapeutic environment immersed with peace and purpose. Additionally, by drawing on the Collective Wisdom, you tap into a universal narrative that supports a compassionate, empathetic approach to healing, enhancing the collective well-being of those you serve.

As we close this chapter, our curiosity turns toward the vital essence of life itself. The next chapter unfolds the mystery of vitality: the life-force energy. Are you ready to unlock the secrets to a more vibrant existence?

Chapter 5

KEY #5 —VITALITY
Cultivating a Bond
with Life-Force Energy

Before You Begin, Download These Resources:

*"Invoking Sacred Purification" guided visualization audio and
the "Vitality Planner" form in color.*

https://beaconout.com/bsr

The pain in my foot was so sharp and sudden that it surprised me. Catching my breath, I tried to understand what's going on. I didn't fall. I was not injured. What is going on? I had to limp into the chair and sit down to gather my thoughts.

It was the day we moved to our new apartment in Atlanta in 2022. The movers brought in the boxes and furniture from the truck. My role was simple—tell them where to place each piece.

But there was something else that happened that day.

I received a text message from a friend 15 minutes before the pain started. It said: "I'm in terrible condition. The doctor says I'm dying. Please send Reiki."

So, I did. I stopped everything and sent her remote Reiki.

Her text should not have been a surprise. As her health had deteriorated over the last few months, we'd communicated regularly. Whenever she was in pain and had another health scare, she'd text me and ask for Reiki. An hour or two later, she'd text me back: "The Reiki helped. I feel much better."

This time was different. She had never before used the word "dying."

Receiving my friend's message in a vulnerable moment shocked me. It was two days after we had said goodbye to our apartment in Brooklyn and watched the truck with our belongings drive away. I felt increasingly "homeless" on the two-day drive to Atlanta. Even though I was excited about the move, the demands of the previous few days had taken a toll on me.

When we got the key that morning, the truck was already outside the building. With insufficient time to process being in our new apartment, I was exhausted and a bit lost.

By the time the movers left, I couldn't walk. The pain was too intense. I lay down and shifted my awareness inward. As soon as I connected with life-force energy and allowed it to recharge me, I felt a massive relief. Then came the clarity:

My pain was a response to my friend's message.

I was not full enough to manage my emotions. And with no appropriate space to digest the news, I was an energetic container leaking life-force. I was exhausted physically and emotionally. My energy well was empty.

I pushed down the emotions and got numb.

I dropped into an automatic response that every empath can easily recognize: taking on somebody else's pain, feeling worse, while they feel better.

The sensitive girl within me felt homeless and lost. We just said goodbye to seven years of living in New York. She needed love. I needed someone to take care of ME. The natural giver within me did the only thing she knew—do whatever she could to make the other person feel better. There were no filters or boundaries. Without going through a healthy process of digesting the news and feeling the emotions, I could not deal with the situation from an empowered place. I couldn't do what I usually do—connect with the universal energy, ground, recharge, and raise my vibration. With me not self-leading the process as usual, my body had only one solution: gifting me with a pain that forced me to stop and deal with my emotions and exhaustion.

My supportive husband was okay with us not starting to unpack like we planned. He left to get coffee, and gave me space to heal.

I only took a few minutes to see the broader picture and understand what happened.

I made three calls. The first two were to Dawn and Rachel, my team members, who immediately began sending me remote Reiki. The third call was to my friend who had sent the message. I knew speaking with her was a crucial step in healing. I didn't share what had happened to me. Instead, I asked how she was feeling. I wasn't surprised when she said, "The Reiki you sent today worked like a miracle. It's the first time in days that I've been able to eat and walk. I feel so much better!"

I received my confirmation. I had taken on my friend's pain. I felt worse. She felt better.

Another clarity emerged: My friend's neuropathy limited her ability to walk. Her legs were in tremendous pain. It's no wonder that taking on her pain manifested physically in my leg and stopped me from walking. Talking to my friend on the phone allowed me to energetically return some of her energy that I had absorbed while reclaiming my own.

Here I was gaining clarity about things that are fundamental to me. We never teach what we don't need to learn, right? The fact that many of the women I mentor and teach are highly sensitive to energy didn't protect me from facing one of my spiritual lessons about the importance of setting boundaries and self-care, especially when dealing with the energy of others.

I can humbly state that in the past 20 years, occurrences of extreme situations where life-force leaks resulted in physical pain in my body have been a rare exception. Such incidents happened more frequently before I became an expert in energy work.

This experience taught me a powerful lesson about our energies' interconnectedness and the need to continuously set energetic boundaries, especially when we are not well.

> *Addressing the leaks in our life-force—a metaphor for managing energy loss—and recharging with vital energy is crucial for maintaining a vibrant, energetic state of being. It's essential to manage our energy and clear away emotional clutter to unlock our fullest capabilities.*

Now, let's take a step back and gain a deeper understanding of the consequences and solutions for leaks in life-force energy and failure to regulate the nervous system.

What is Life-Force Energy?

All of existence is energy. Every thought, feeling, and action we experience is a form of energy. Our bodies are made up of energy that vibrates at specific frequencies, making us alive and connected.

Often attributed to Albert Einstein, "Everything is energy, and that is all there is to it," captures the essence of his groundbreaking concept of the relationship between mass and energy, presented through the famous equation $E=mc^2$, which demonstrates this. In simpler terms, energy cannot be created or destroyed; it can only be transformed from one form to another. This highlights the importance of understanding the energy surrounding us and how we can harness it to create positive change in our lives and the world around us.

When our body's energetic system is disrupted, physical symptoms can appear in the body and affect our overall well-being.

Life-force energy is believed to be the energy that flows through all living things, and it can be measured in humans and animals by their overall vitality.

It is thought to be the essence of life that connects us all and gives us our sense of purpose. Think of it as an invisible power that connects us to the bigger picture of the universe.

The terms *prana, qi,* and *chi* are often used interchangeably with life-force energy, as they all refer to the same concept. Prana is the Sanskrit word for "life-force" or "vital principle," while qi or chi refers to an active principle forming part of any living thing, which translates to "natural energy."

When vital energy flows freely throughout the body, it leads to physical, mental, and emotional health. It also allows us to become more open and connected with ourselves and others.

Our bodies are constantly absorbing and releasing energy. When we are depleted or lacking life-force, it can manifest in physical symptoms such as fatigue, illness, or even depression.

By recognizing when we are running low on life-force and taking proactive steps to restore balance, we can prevent further depletion and create a healthier version of ourselves.

> *Life-force energy is vital to our physical, emotional, and spiritual well-being. However, many of us may unknowingly leak our life-force energy, resulting in various imbalances and illnesses.*
>
> *We are energetic beings, continuously absorbing energy from others and our surroundings throughout the day. It is our sacred responsibility to care for ourselves diligently, ensuring that we remain in harmony with the natural flow of life's vitality.*

Why We Leak Life-Force

Both in my practice and within the pages of this book, I explore the pathways of life-force, seeking not just to understand but to harmonize with its rhythms. My journey has revealed that when we are in sync with this energy, we are in sync with life. And yet, it is not uncommon for us to experience "leaks"—moments where our energy dissipates, lost to the countless distractions and emotional disruptions we face.

One of the reasons we leak life-force energy is due to unresolved emotions and traumas. When we encounter difficult experiences in life, our bodies may hold onto the energetic excess of that experience. This can lead to blockages and disruptions in the flow of life-force energy, resulting in various health issues and emotional imbalances.

You may be asking yourself how holding onto trauma can lead to leaking life-force. Imagine a balloon filled with water; if the water represents the traumatic energy and the balloon represents your energy field, any additional water increases pressure on the balloon's surface. Over time, this constant pressure and extra weight can create small holes, or "leaks," through which life-force energy may escape, much like water dripping from a stressed and overburdened balloon.

Our energy can weaken for many other reasons. It might happen when we're stressed, not sleeping well, feeling unwell, hear upsetting news, have trouble in our relationships, or are overwhelmed by too much work, just to name a few examples.

Life's demands, with all their various roles and responsibilities, can sometimes feel overwhelming, leaving you exhausted not just by the end of the day, but sometimes just a few hours after it starts. Adding to this a constant inner dialogue of negative thoughts, a pessimistic mindset, and the habit of pushing down your emotions can also drain your vitality. All these factors can significantly contribute to the depletion of your life-force energy.

Stress can also trigger a fight-or-flight state in the body, leading to a buildup of energetic tension and further blockages in the flow of life-force energy. These blockages are similar to debris blocking a river's path. When the natural flow is obstructed, the river doesn't stop; instead, it finds alternate routes, often spilling over or seeping out of its natural course. In the same way, energetic blockages from stress redirect life-force energy, causing it to "leak" out through less optimal paths, which may manifest as diminished vitality or health.

Unhealthy lifestyle choices, such as poor diet, lack of exercise, and substance abuse, can also cause us to leak our life-force energy. These habits place stress on the body, leading to imbalances in our energy systems.

In contrast, adopting healthy practices, such as regular exercise, a nutrient-dense diet, and mindfulness practices like meditation, can help to boost and restore our life-force energy.

> Restoring balance, harmony, and well-being centers on recognizing and addressing the root causes of energy imbalances and understanding how life-force energy circulates within our body.

Interconnected Energy: The Science and Spirituality of Our Universal Matrix

Lynn McTaggart's book *The Field: The Quest for the Secret Force of the Universe* introduces the concept of the Zero Point Field, an underlying energy matrix that suggests the universe is interconnected.

Her synthesis of scientific research suggests that our bodies are not isolated entities but part of a vast network of energy exchanges. This perspective supports my work's concept that a "leak" in an individual's energy can have broader implications within this universal matrix.

McTaggart discusses the potent influence of consciousness on health and the environment, reinforcing the notion that our thoughts and intentions hold power over the physical realm. Such insights resonate with the themes of my work, especially the importance of maintaining our life-force energy to ensure well-being. My idea of "leaking energy" aligns with her observations that negative mental states can cut our harmonious connection to the Zero Point Field, manifesting as various health disturbances.

McTaggart's work suggests that engaging with the Field through intentional practices could be vital to restoring our energetic balance, offering a scientific foundation for the restorative practices I advocate for, such as Reiki and mindfulness.

In his work *The Untethered Soul* and other writings, Michael Singer discusses letting go of the mental and emotional blocks that lead us to lesser versions of ourselves. His teachings emphasize the importance of releasing inner resistance, which could be seen metaphorically as a form of "energy leak."

To my understanding, the reason inner resistance can be seen as a form of energy leak is because it consumes our mental and emotional resources. Resistance often uses a significant amount of our life-force to maintain psychological defenses or to sustain ongoing internal conflicts. This effort to oppose our natural flow of emotions and experiences is like a dam in a river, where water pressure builds up and starts to find other ways to escape. Over time, this pressure can lead to cracks or openings in the dam, symbolizing how persistent inner resistance can cause our vital energy to seep away, leaving us feeling drained and less vibrant.

Singer often speaks about the flow of energy through the spiritual heart and how blockages due to clinging to past pains or fears can lead to emotional and psychological distress.

The main pathways through which life-force energy flows into and out of our body are the *meridians*, the *aura*, and the *chakras*.

> " *Working with a person's energetic pathways—including the meridians, the aura, and the chakra system—allows us to restore balance and create a healthier life. Once we understand these patterns, we can work to clear blockages, restore the natural flow of energy, and come back into alignment with ourselves.* "

Meridians: The Circulatory Channels of Life-Force Energy

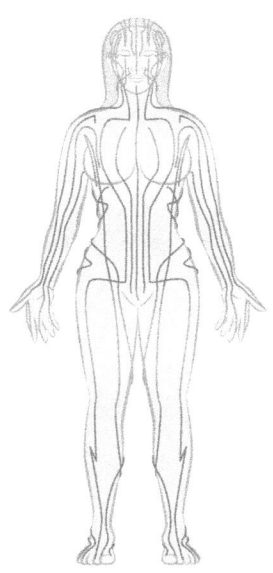

The concept of meridians is a cornerstone of traditional Chinese medicine. Meridians are energy pathways that connect the surface of our body with deep internal organs and systems. These pathways serve as the main road for the flow of qi or life-force energy, ensuring the body's energetic ecosystem remains in dynamic equilibrium. Just like rivers that nourish the land through which they flow, meridians channel vital energy to every nook and cranny of the body. When these channels are free from obstruction, energy circulates with ease, fostering health and vitality. However should blockages arise—just like a dam obstructing a river's flow—physical and emotional imbalances may occur.

The 12 primary meridians from which qi (life-force energy) enters and exits the body can be divided into *yin* (inhaling) and *yang* (exhaling).

" Deepening our understanding of meridian pathways can enhance our ability to navigate the complex interplay between our environment and internal health, allowing us to apply targeted practices that dissolve blockages and restore harmonious energy flow. "

Aura: The Reflective Energy Field

Aura refers to a subtle field surrounding each individual that reflects their emotional state at any given time. This field is made up of positive and negative particles, which create an energetic vibration. It is believed that this aura plays a significant role in determining a person's physical and emotional health since it acts as a filter to allow specific energies into our system, while blocking others out.

When we are healthy and balanced, our aura radiates light, which allows more life-force energy to flow freely throughout us, giving us greater vitality and well-being. On the other hand, when we feel stressed or overwhelmed, this same aura contracts, resulting in an imbalance within ourselves, leading eventually to physical illness if left unchecked for long enough periods.

The aura acts as a living, breathing canvas that reflects the complex story of our inner state. Much like a mood ring changes color with our body's temperature, our aura shifts and morphs in response to

our emotions, thoughts, and overall well-being. This radiant ring is not just a passive reflection; it is an active participant in our interactions with the world around us. It absorbs and repels energies, protects us from external influences, and can even communicate with the auras of others. As an advocate for Reiki as a daily practice for vitality, I can testify that individuals who regularly practice Reiki often develop a natural sensitivity in their hands, enabling them to sense and work with people's auras effectively.

> " A vibrant, expansive aura can attract positivity and repel negativity, serving as a shield and a beacon. Learning to sense and visualize our aura, to cleanse and fortify it, can be a profound tool in our journey toward wellness, acting as both a diagnostic indicator and a therapeutic agent. "

Chakras: Centers of Spiritual and Physical Health

Chakras, meaning "wheel of light" in Sanskrit, are energy centers situated around our spinal cord, each connected to various organs and aspects of our being. These vortices transmit *qi* (life-force energy) throughout our body, regulating the intake and expulsion of energy to maintain balance and health.

Each chakra is uniquely associated with an element, color, emotion, physical organ, and spiritual power, all of which are crucial for our overall equilibrium. Disharmony in any chakra, due to blockages or imbalance, can manifest as physical or emotional ailments, affecting our experience of life.

By engaging with our chakras through practices like Reiki, meditation, and yoga, we can restore balance across these energy centers. This harmonization plays a key role in how we process emotions, experience reality, and connect with the spiritual territory.

> " A balanced chakra system enhances our interactions with the world and deepens our connection to the self and the divine. On the other hand, blockages can cause disturbances that impact our well-being. Therefore, working with chakras is vital for living a balanced and aligned life, both physically and spiritually. "

Balancing Pathways: Practical Application

It is believed that the meridians, chakras, and aura dysfunction can occur before a physical disease manifests in the body.

Working with these energetic layers has the potential for diagnostic, preventative, and treatment purposes. Many practitioners believe that these approaches have significant potential for treating physical ailments.

As professionals, we must find practices that suit our needs and promote energy flow. Such practices can include acupressure or acupuncture, qigong and tai chi, mindfulness and breathwork, sound healing, and yoga. While this discussion of energetic pathways is brief, I encourage you to explore this more deeply and discover practices that resonate with you. This will enhance your well-being by supporting an open and harmonious flow within your energetic body.

On a personal note, the foundational practice that I have been embracing, teaching, and incorporating into my life since 1996 is Reiki. I begin and conclude each day with a self-Reiki session. The self-Reiki treatment offers a practical method to align with life-force energy and effectively address energy leaks. Reiki serves as a self-care practice that promotes healing and spiritually enriches us by channeling the pure universal energy our bodies require to restore balance and function optimally.

A remarkable aspect of Reiki is its harmonious integration with other practices. It functions as a unifying element, enhancing various modalities with its cohesive energy.

I do not consider Reiki to be superior to other practices. Indeed, I actively participate in many of them myself. My emphasis on Reiki stems from its profound transformative influence on my life, laying the groundwork for my spiritual journey and self-care routine more than any other modality I have practiced since 1996.

If you don't already have a daily practice like Reiki, or other methods that help you reset, recharge, or restore your life-force energy, it's worth exploring some that you may want to incorporate into your routine.

Recognizing the complex web of energy pathways that rule our well-being is just the beginning.

> " *Through daily, intentional practices, we can apply this understanding to cultivate and maintain vitality. For professionals committed to thriving in their fields, establishing routines at the start and end of the day, and in between work sessions is essential for preserving and protecting this vital energy.* "

Morning Rituals: Awakening with Intention

Morning routines set the tone for the day. Initiating the day with intentional practices to charge our meridians, aura, and chakras with pure, life-force energy, ensures we start our day aligned and energized.

Evening Wind-Down: Releasing the Day's Energy

Similarly, evening routines are about decompressing and clearing any accumulated stress. Using clearing and protecting techniques to cleanse our aura and soothe our chakras promotes restorative sleep and healing.

In Between: Re-Setting and Re-Energizing During Breaks

The time between work sessions holds as much importance as the work itself. Use these breaks effectively to recharge and reset. This could mean stepping away from your workspace, engaging in quick physical activities like stretching or brisk walking, or practicing brief mindfulness exercises. I've observed many professionals who arrange consecutive appointments with clients without scheduling any breaks for renewal. They often wonder why they're completely exhausted by the day's end. Back-to-back scheduling can make you feel like you've lost control of your day and diminish performance over time. Nutrition also carries significant weight in maintaining energy levels. Consuming balanced meals and ensuring proper daily hydration can help stave off energy slumps.

> *Establishing morning, evening, and in-between practices isn't just routine; it's a transformative discipline crucial for maintaining energetic equilibrium. It fosters a harmony that resonates through our entire being, making it equally important to nurture our emotional landscape as we do our physical spaces.*

Feeling Fully: The Role of Emotion in Sustaining Life-Force Energy

We must also address our emotional state as we nurture our life-force energy.

In the rhythm of our workdays, where we diligently recharge our energy through mindful breaks and nourishing activities, there lies another vital practice often overlooked: the mindful acknowledgment and processing of our emotions. This practice is not separate from our routines but is integral to sustaining our vitality.

> *Remember that you are not only a professional; you are also human.*

Part of your humanness is experiencing solid emotions when helping other people. Part of your humanness is also to do whatever it takes to avoid feeling the pain, unless you're aware that it is not a best practice to do that.

As Brené Brown—a renowned researcher and storyteller who focuses on vulnerability, courage, and empathy—often points out, humans are wired to avoid pain, sometimes even at the cost of causing pain to others. It's a natural defense mechanism that can lead to disconnection from our true selves and those we serve.

In her book *Atlas of the Heart*, Brené Brown explores the emotions that shape our experiences and influence our interactions with others. She encourages us to embrace vulnerability and explore our emotional landscapes with curiosity and compassion. Brown emphasizes that we can foster greater empathy for ourselves and connect more deeply with others by understanding the depths and nuances of our feelings. Her work invites us to become mapmakers of our emotional world, recognizing that acknowledging and naming our emotions is a decisive step toward wholehearted living and sustaining our life-force energy.

Brené Brown's insights remind us of the importance of facing our emotions head-on, without armor, to connect and heal truly.

This is especially relevant since trauma is part of the human experience, and we all encounter it on some level. *It is not uncommon for your trauma to get triggered while you help people heal.* While your default, like many of us, may be to suppress the emotions—and if you live a spiritual life, you may even unknowingly use spirituality to bypass the feelings—it is crucial to keep practices in place to help you feel the emotions, and give them love and compassion.

> *How we navigate our inner emotional landscape sets the foundation for our resilience and clarity. It empowers us to stand as pillars of support for others while honoring the integrity of our path.*

Why Nurturing Vitality and Emotional Resilience Is Key for Professional Fulfillment

> *Imagine an artist at work on a canvas. They need the 'right distance' to appreciate the entirety of their work and ensure no detail is overlooked. This perspective is crucial, not just in art but in our professional roles as well.*

As you prepare to assist others in their soulful journeys, consider this: much like the artist, you must cultivate *"energetic fitness."* This is your metaphorical gym, where you strengthen your ability to maintain the optimal distance from your work—*close enough to be empathetic, yet far enough to remain regulated and helpful.*

Through years of guiding and mentoring professionals, I've observed four predominant tendencies that can compromise our energetic health:

1. Placing others' needs above our own, mastering the art of giving love but failing to reserve it for ourselves

2. Gravitating naturally toward the role of fixer or rescuer, often to the damage of our boundaries

3. Absorbing the emotions and distress of others, leading to a blurred line between personal and professional feelings

4. Not creating the "right distance" and becoming too emotionally involved, potentially clouding our judgment and leading to a loss of professional effectiveness

To start building strong vitality, we've got to be aware. We should recognize what's stopping us from staying full of energy. Look at those four natural tendencies I talked about—do any of them sound like you? Maybe you're the type who always wants to fix things, or perhaps you find yourself taking on what your clients feel without even realizing it. Or is there another pattern you've noticed in yourself that's draining your energy?

Knowing what's going on is the first step. Once you spot where your energy is slipping away, you can start figuring out how to hold onto it—maybe on your own, or with a little help. Sticking to a daily practice to keep your energy up is extremely important. But remember, even if you're doing everything right, there will be times when you end up giving more than receiving. When that happens, it's a signal to take a step back. Stop, recharge, and give yourself a chance to see things with fresh eyes.

I've witnessed numerous professionals who have received clear signals from their bodies indicating the need for a pause and reset, yet they didn't give themselves permission to take the necessary break.

Eventually, their situation escalated to the point where they had no choice but to stop and focus on self-care.

> *Don't wait until circumstances compel you to act. It's crucial to proactively take care of yourself and establish energetic boundaries, enabling you to serve effectively.*

Soulful Snapshot

Take Carol, for example, an EMDR (Eye Movement Desensitization and Reprocessing) therapist and licensed clinical social worker who specializes in trauma work and has over three decades of experience. Despite her extensive background, she began to suffer from unexplained headaches, back and leg pain, fluctuating blood sugar levels, and constant fatigue after 27 years in her field. Medical examinations revealed no clear cause of her ailments. It wasn't until she participated in my Reiki training that Carol recognized these symptoms as manifestations of her depleted life-force energy. By adopting a daily routine of self-treatment energy work, she soon regained her vitality and rediscovered the joy in her life that had been missing. When Carol completed the training and graduated as a Reiki Master, she started integrating energy work with her talk therapy and EMDR sessions.

"Boosting my life-force energy daily has sharpened my mind, improved my health, and elevated my professional practice. It's enabled me to offer better service to my clients," Carol shared. Her health improved, resolving her persistent issues once she addressed the depletion of her life-force energy. Moreover, she began instructing her clients on managing and replenishing their energy.

Carol's professional growth included teaching her clients to identify and repair leaks in their life-force and to incorporate self-administered Reiki into their routines. Reflecting on the integration of energy work into her practice over the years, Carol observed that her clients experience deeper and faster healing, with more long-term transformations, underscoring the lasting impact of energy work in therapeutic practices.

Earlier, we discussed certain common tendencies among professionals—like putting others' needs first, trying to fix everything, taking on other people's emotions, and not keeping the right emotional distance. Carol's story is a clear reminder of why it's critical to be aware of these patterns in ourselves. Recognizing these tendencies is pivotal to understanding why nurturing our vitality and emotional resilience is key to professional fulfillment.

We need to actively counteract these inclinations to safeguard our well-being, preserve our capacity to serve others effectively, and fully engage in our professional and personal lives. By promoting vitality, we power our ability to perform and provide care. By developing emotional resilience, we build the strength to meet the challenges of our work head-on, without losing sight of who we are.

Carol's journey vividly demonstrates the transformative power of self-care. Now, she concludes her week with a Reiki session, rather than a "talk-therapy" session, ensuring she starts her weekend recharged and in equilibrium, in stark contrast to her past, where weekends were for recuperation from weekly fatigue. This shift is a powerful endorsement of self-care, showing that it is essential not only for personal well-being but also as a means to elevate one's professional practice.

Since 1996, I've been practicing, teaching, and living Reiki—it's a big part of who I am. I connect with Carol's story deeply. Time and again, I've seen how bringing Reiki into my sessions, even remotely through a screen, shields me from losing my own energy. I don't just use my own strength; I tap into the universal force, letting that life-force energy pass from me to someone else. This doesn't just help the person receiving it; it keeps me balanced too and preserves my energy. And on those rare days when I do feel a bit empty after a session, a quick self-Reiki treatment is all it takes to bring me right back to center.

" *In the dance of giving and receiving, fostering our vitality, cultivating emotional resilience, and tending to our own energetic health is not just an act of self-care—it's a cornerstone of professional practice. These practices fuel our capacity to work and care, ensuring that we thrive through the challenges of our roles without losing sight of ourselves.* "

Soulful Exercise: Designing Your Monthly Vitality Plan

Taking control of your energy and emotional well-being is an active process that requires commitment and conscious decision-making. Each month, you can reflect on the practices that serve you and those that you may need to adjust. To facilitate this, I encourage you to use the "Vitality Planner" presented in this chapter as a tool for intentional living and self-care.

Instructions for Completing Your Monthly Vitality Planner:

1. *Reflect on the Past Month:* Before you begin planning for the upcoming month, take a moment to reflect on the practices you've used. Ask yourself: Which routines provided the most energy? Which ones didn't serve you as well?

2. *Evaluate Your Current Practices:* Review your morning, evening, and in-between practices. Note any changes in how you felt over the month—more energized, balanced, or strained.

3. *Consider New Exercises:* Look at the list of exercises provided below. Are there any new practices you feel drawn to? Are you curious to try it?

4. *Fill Out Your Vitality Planner:* With the insights from your reflection, fill out your planner for the new month. Decide if you want to continue with the same practices or introduce new ones. Be specific about what you will do and when you will do it.

5. *Set Clear Intentions:* For each practice you choose, set an intention. What do you hope to achieve with this practice? How will it contribute to your vitality?

6. *Commit to Consistency:* Consistency is critical to seeing the benefits of any practice. Commit to your chosen routines for the month ahead. Mark them in your planner as appointments with yourself that must be noticed.

7. *Plan for Evaluation:* At the end of the month, revisit your Vitality Planner to assess what's working and what isn't. Set a reminder for this evaluation, ensuring it's a non-negotiable part of your routine.

Remember, the goal is to find what works best for you and helps you maintain high vitality. It's about personalizing your approach to self-care and energy management.

A Selection of Exercises for Optimal Vitality

These practices can be incorporated into your monthly Vitality Planner for energy clearing, recharging, and resetting:

1. *Self-Reiki or Other Energy Healing Modality Session.* Channel healing energy through your body using Reiki or another energy healing practice.

2. *Yoga Postures.* Perform a series of yoga postures to align your physical and energetic body.

3. *Meditation with Intention.* Meditate and set a clear intention to guide your energy throughout the day.

4. *Protection Bubble Visualization.* Visualize a protective bubble of light around you for energetic protection.

5. *Triple Gratitude Reflection.* Reflect on three positive experiences that happened that day. Make them specific for maximum impact.

6. *Energy Clearing Visualization.* Imagine a ball of light moving through your body, clearing and revitalizing your energy.

7. *Intentional Movement.* Engage in movement such as walking, stretching, practicing qigong, tai chi, or dancing to music you love to reconnect with your body and release tension.

8. *Protective Imagery.* Use symbols of protection, like a Star of David, a cross, or other symbols that resonate with you, as barriers to negative energy.

9. *Energetic Curtain.* Picture a light curtain around you as a shield from unwanted energies.

10. *Positive Mantra Recitation.* Use affirming mantras such as "Healed, whole and complete" or "Cleared, energized and safe" to maintain a positive and high vibrational state.

11. *Grounding Techniques.* Practice grounding exercises like visualizing roots growing from your feet into the earth or walking mindfully on natural ground.

12. *Breathing Exercises.* Use simple breathing techniques, like deep abdominal breathing or alternate nostril breathing, to center and calm your energy.

As you fill out your Vitality Planner, consider these exercises and additional exercises of your choice. Select those that resonate with you. Adapt your plan each month to meet your individual energy management needs and preferences.

Now that we have explored "around-the-clock Soul-care," let's deepen our experience with a guided visualization.

After exploring the profound interconnectedness of our life-force energy and recognizing the importance of self-care and boundaries, let's now transition into a space of healing and rejuvenation. Join me in a guided visualization to cleanse your energy and strengthen your divine connection, inviting peace and vitality to flow through you.

VITALITY PLANNER

Name	Date	Intention

☀	⧖	☾
MORNING RITUALS	**IN-BETWEEN**	**EVENING WIND-DOWN**

NOTES & REFLECTION

Guided Visualization:
Invoking Sacred Purification

This guided visualization is designed to help you cleanse your energy and strengthen your connection to the divine. It's a journey of release and renewal intended to clear your energetic field and align you with the higher frequencies of love and light.

When you are ready to begin the journey, find a comfortable position, take a deep breath, and listen to the audio you've downloaded, which is transcribed below.

Begin by settling into the present moment, shifting your awareness from any external distractions to allow yourself the fullness of this moment.

Relax your body, releasing tension from your shoulders and softening your facial muscles. Open your heart and sense the support of the earth beneath you and the divine above.

Inhale deeply through your nose, drawing the breath down to your stomach, keeping your chest still. As you exhale through your lips, engage your abdominal muscles, gently guiding the breath out, releasing all that no longer serves you.

Inhale again, this time visualizing a radiant white light entering with your breath, symbolizing love, compassion, gentleness, and tenderness. Exhale worry, tension, pain, and concern, allowing all that is not serving you to be released.

With each breath in, let the white light fill you, cleansing and purifying from the inside out. With each breath out, feel lighter, more open.

Now, bring your awareness to the crown of your head. Envision a bright white fountain of light coming from above, entering through the crown chakra. Feel it washing over your entire being, flowing through your body to the very soles of your feet. This fountain of light purifies your physical form, clearing away the burdens from your shoulders and the weights of responsibility and stress, gently dissolving all heaviness around your heart and soothing any emotional or energetic discomfort.

Allow this divine fountain to expand, creating a shimmering field around you and purifying your aura. Visualize this energy, washing away old emotions, pain, or suffering you've collected, leaving you cleansed, refreshed, and light.

As this process unfolds, imagine forming a vertical connection. Your lower body grows roots that grow deep into the earth, anchoring you with stability and nourishment. As you ground down, your upper body lifts, reaching for the sky, basking in the celestial glow, connecting you to the divine.

Shift your focus to the soles of your feet and imagine invisible cords extending from them deep into the earth's core. Feel the nurturing embrace of Mother Earth as these cords anchor you firmly to her. Allow yourself to be supported and held by this connection. Envision the grounding energy of the earth rising through these cords, filling your entire being—upward and outward—infusing every cell of your body with stability and vitality.

Once you feel grounded and cleansed internally and externally, visualize a bubble wrapping you. This bubble can be touched with the soft hues of pink for love and white for purity.

Rest within your bubble and allow yourself to be receptive to the divine light and healing energies that flow through this meditation. Give yourself permission to fully receive, surrender to the light, and be open to the love that is being offered to you right now.

Place your hands over your heart, and gently repeat the following mantra:

> Be with your heart first,
> Root down to the earth,
> Rise up to the divine,
> Be a lighthouse.

Feel the vertical connection solidify as you root down and rise up, becoming a beacon of light, a lighthouse within the flow of life.

When you're ready, gently bring your awareness back to the present moment, carrying with you the vertical connection and being mindful of your emotions as you open your eyes.

Reflect on the Chapter: Questions to Consider

1. Consider the idea of "energy leaks." What situations or emotions tend to drain your vitality the most?

2. Reflect on the concept of "energy sources." What activities, situations, or emotions tend to boost your vitality and bring you a sense of rejuvenation?

3. How do you maintain boundaries between absorbing others' emotions and preserving your own emotional well-being?

4. In what ways could adopting the practices suggested in this chapter change your professional effectiveness and personal fulfillment?

5. As you consider the practices and insights from this chapter, what is one commitment you're willing to make toward cultivating your vitality and emotional resilience?

From Words to Action: Applying This Chapter's Lessons

To embrace vitality is to commit to a series of conscious actions that enrich our professional lives and personal well-being.

Begin with a self-assessment of your energy. What drains you? What energizes you? Then, integrate the practices that resonate with you into your routine, engaging them with intention and mindfulness.

Once a month, take the time to reflect on your current practices. Assess their effectiveness and consider whether it's time to introduce new techniques from your library. This is not about being rigid but about remaining fluid and responsive to your needs. Your morning, evening, and inter-session rituals should be living routines that adapt as you do.

The Vitality Planner becomes a canvas where you paint your monthly energy blueprint. It's a living document, inviting regular reflection and fine-tuning. Dedicate time each month to revisit this planner, treating it as a strategic session with yourself to gauge the efficacy of your chosen practices.

Take an active role in the process of cultivating a living practice that adapts and grows with you as you deepen your bond with life-force energy.

Unfolding the Next Layer

Reflecting on our exploration of vitality, we have journeyed through understanding life-force energy, uncovering the pathways of its flow and recognizing the importance of nurturing our energetic essence. We've learned that the lows and highs of our inner energy deeply affect the quality of our professional and personal lives.

> *It is wise to maintain a dynamic library of tools, rituals, and techniques dedicated to clearing, protecting, and energizing your being to build vitality and manage your energy. Think of it as a personal toolkit that evolves with you—a collection of practices that resonates with your current state and supports your growth.*

Developing and maintaining morning, evening, and in-between session routines and regularly revisiting your Vitality Planner each month provides a solid framework to cultivate and sustain your vitality, ensuring a balanced and energized personal and professional existence.

None of this is sustainable without true embodiment. What does it mean to embody our experiences? How does this deepen our connection to the healing power within? The next chapter invites us to explore these questions, guiding us to embrace our bodies as the ultimate conduits to the Soul's wisdom.

Chapter 6

KEY # 6—EMBODIMENT
Embracing the Body
as a Gateway to the Soul

Before You Begin, Download This Resource:
"Grounding in the Now" guided visualization audio.

https://beaconout.com/bsr

I had always dreamed of having a house full of children.

In the sixth month of my first pregnancy, I found myself hospitalized due to severe bleeding. What began as a time of joy swiftly shifted into sorrow when I prematurely went into labor and experienced the loss of our first baby. Tragically, this heartache was not a solitary event; it repeated itself six times over eight pregnancies. Each case of early labor and the following loss dropped me deeper into a hole of grief that felt unbearable. The termination of my final pregnancy marked the peak of my trauma since the procedure was challenging, to say the least.

Even though those times were tough, I was blessed with two wonderful children. Their vibrant, intelligent, and creative spirits bring me joy. I love being a mother, and I love being their mother. Nevertheless, the pain of losing six pregnancies continued to cast a shadow over me.

After my husband and I chose to stop trying to expand our family further, I was mentally prepared to leave behind the sorrow associated with the babies I lost and concentrate on nurturing the incredible children in my care. While my mind was set on moving past this, my body lingered in a state of unrest. Nightmares and vivid recollections of the traumas endured during the pregnancies and labors haunted me. Every attempt to shed the grief and embrace joy was met with a physiological response—cold sweats, digestive issues, episodes of vertigo, and persistent pain. These physical setbacks left me in a state of depression, hindering the healing that my mind yearned for. Many of my physical symptoms couldn't be explained by traditional Western medicine.

After understanding the limitations of talk therapy and deciding to pursue holistic ways to heal, it was the physical, energetic shifts I experienced through my studies—Reiki, shiatsu, kundalini meditation, reflexology, color therapy, and intentional movement, to name a few—that allowed me to heal deeply.

I finally understood that the trauma I hadn't dealt with was causing my physical issues.

Words did not provide a "safe enough" path to healing for me, but I found sanctuary and recovery in the healing of my body.

The pivotal shift in my journey unfolded with a single understanding that opened my eyes to new possibilities and a new understanding:

> " *The fundamental challenge for people who have suffered trauma is to cultivate a reliable sense of safety in their own bodies.* "

Understanding Trauma: Moving Beyond Talk Therapy

Bessel van der Kolk, a renowned psychiatrist and a pioneering researcher in the field of trauma, underscores a profound truth in his influential work *The Body Keeps the Score: Brain, Mind, and Body in the Healing of Trauma.* He illuminates the often-overlooked reality that individuals who have experienced trauma may live in a continuous state of alert, as if the trauma were still happening in the present. His extensive research reveals how trauma leaves an indelible imprint on our bodies, leading to a host of physical and emotional challenges. Van der Kolk's insights have been pivotal in the understanding that true healing requires addressing the stored trauma within the body, and fostering a sense of safety is the cornerstone of this transformative journey.

Trying to address my childhood and adult trauma with a therapist who was not trauma-informed unlocked a deeper mission for me. After testing many different healing modalities over the years and developing proven techniques, I've designed a more holistic approach to trauma healing.

None of us willingly choose to experience trauma, yet we are all susceptible to its effects. It is an inevitable part of the human experience. By acknowledging this truth, we can gain a deeper appreciation for the significance of our healing.

As professionals, we must recognize the profound impact of trauma on mental health and well-being.

Our professionalism is essential when assisting individuals in their healing journey. Given the increasing awareness about trauma, we must adopt trauma-informed approaches responsibly. Doing so ensures that we do not unintentionally cause further harm or retraumatize ourselves and others. I often come across energy healers discussing blocked energy and psychic attachments, but they overlook a fundamental truth: Unaddressed trauma triggers these issues.

Trauma is a term used to describe any event or accumulation of adverse experiences, large or small, that results in an intense emotional impact on a person. Trauma can range from physical violence, such as an assault, to emotional abuse caused by neglect or abandonment. Natural disasters, serious illnesses, and accidents can also cause it.

In our exploration of trauma and its profound impact on the body and soul, it's important to acknowledge just how common these experiences are. The "Adverse Childhood Experiences Study," led by Vincent Felitti, M.D., and Robert Anda, M.D., revealed a startling statistic: Approximately 75% of the population has experienced at least one traumatic event. This illustrates that trauma is not an isolated phenomenon; it touches the lives of many people.

Moreover, the way trauma manifests can vary significantly from one person to another, reinforcing the need for personalized approaches to healing. Recognizing the diversity of trauma's impact, the American Psychiatric Association updated the *Diagnostic and Statistical Manual of Mental Disorders* in 2022 to include conditions such as prolonged grief disorder and to provide specific codes for behaviors related to trauma, such as suicidal actions and non-suicidal self-injury. This update also aims to be more inclusive, addressing the historical impact of racial discrimination in clinical diagnoses.

Understanding that trauma is not always a singular event is crucial. Developmental trauma, like experiencing neglect or having emotionally absent parents, can lead to a cascade of psychological, physical, and behavioral issues that persist into adulthood. This information not only broadens our understanding of trauma but also validates the experiences of those who suffer from its long-term effects.

> *In the wake of trauma, the path to recovery often demands more than just talk therapy; it requires a deep, embodied approach known as somatic healing.*

Recognizing the multidimensional nature of trauma opens the door to a more nuanced healing approach. Beyond conventional talk therapy lies the transformative power of practices that engage body and mind. With this foundation, we move toward demystifying two critical mind–body approaches.

Let's Clear the Confusion: Understanding Embodiment and Somatic Healing

In the world of holistic health and therapy, terms like "embodiment" and "somatic healing" can create confusion. It's important to clarify these concepts and understand the differences.

> *Embodiment means being fully present and engaged with our physical existence. It's the conscious experience of inhabiting our bodies and feeling every sensation deeply. It's about recognizing the way our inner life shapes our posture, influences our actions, and is expressed in the way we walk and move.*

Embodiment isn't just about awareness; it's about integration—how thoughts and feelings are integrated into the very structure of our physical being. It's how confidence can straighten our spine, how joy can quicken our steps, and how sorrow can slow our stride. Embodied living is the art of letting our physical self be a true and dynamic expression of our unique individuality.

"Somatic" comes from the Greek word "soma" for "the living body." Somatic healing focuses on the mind–body connection, recognizing that emotional and psychological traumas manifest in our bodily tissues and nervous systems.

> *Somatic healing is an approach to addressing and healing past traumas stored in the body and accessing the whole wisdom of the body for better overall well-being.*

Through techniques like mindful movement, breathwork, and sensory awareness exercises, we and our clients can reconnect with our bodies, often leading to profound shifts in the healing journey.

For professionals, somatic healing is more than a technique; it's a personal practice that helps us maintain our well-being while assisting others. By embodying somatic healing principles, we become attuned to our body's signals, allowing us to navigate our traumas and hold a compassionate space for our clients.

For clients, embodying healing means becoming aware of the cognitive aspects of their trauma and actualizing the healing process within their bodies. *This is the integration of the analytical mind with the emotional body.*

When we, as professionals, model embodiment, we show our clients it's possible to move through the world with safety and "grounded-ness" in their bodies. This can be particularly empowering for those who have felt disassociated from their bodies due to trauma.

By fostering an embodied presence, we offer a blueprint for clients to rebuild trust in their capacity to heal.

We tend to think of the "body" and 'soul" as separate, but healing happens by integrating the two.

> *Embracing our bodies' wisdom opens us to a deeper understanding of healing, not just as a concept but as a lived experience. Genuine embodiment is unlocked not through pure thinking alone but by directing our awareness to our body's sensations and tapping into the embodied knowledge we all possess.*

Embracing Embodiment and Soul Wisdom in Your Work

As a devoted practitioner, you recognize the immeasurable value of incorporating somatic understanding and Soul-work into your practice. Here's how you can practically bring this to life for your clients:

1. *Commit to Your Personal Practice*

Explore not just how your body feels but also the subtle messages from within. Allow your embodiment and somatic practices to be a dialogue with the deeper self. When you create your Vitality Planner, presented in Chapter 5, infuse each activity with an intention to move, feel, connect with, and listen to the whispers of your Soul.

2. *Assess Client Readiness*

In your assessments, encourage clients to perceive their bodies as sacred vessels that house their Souls. Guide them to listen to their body not only for physical cues but also as a means to access their Soul's wisdom. This holistic view can foster a more profound sense of connection and readiness for the transformative work ahead.

3. *Seamlessly Integrate Somatic Tools*

Incorporate somatic tools that facilitate a soulful connection, such as breathwork that invites the breath to move as the spirit, or grounding exercises that encourage clients to feel their body as an anchor for their Soul. By doing so, you help them experience embodiment as a gateway to accessing their Soul's insights.

4. *Nurture Body Awareness*

Guide clients to be aware of their body as a reflection of their Soul. Teach them to observe their physical sensations as messages from the Soul, revealing insights and truths that transcend the cognitive mind. This can open a profound pathway to healing that honors both their human experience and their spiritual essence.

5. *Guide with Skill and Sensitivity*

As you facilitate somatic experiences, do so with respect for the Soul that lives within the body. Be sensitive to the profound revelations that may arise when clients engage deeply with their body's wisdom. Your skillful guidance can help them integrate these insights into a cohesive narrative of healing and self-discovery.

6. *Establish Clear Boundaries*

When exploring the somatic world, be mindful of the sacred space where the body meets the Soul. Ensure that boundaries are set with a deep respect for the client's entire being. For clients with a history of trauma, be particularly cautious and proceed with an informed, trauma-sensitive approach that respects their pace and comfort levels. This creates safety and honors the sacredness of their Soul's journey through healing.

Remember, as a therapist, your embodiment is a beacon for your clients. It shows them that living harmoniously within one's own body is possible.

> Embodying somatic practices extends beyond technique; it represents a deep commitment to honoring the body's wisdom as an essential compass. Acknowledging our bodies as sacred vessels that house our Souls, we embrace a holistic approach, steering us toward a life rich with depth and authenticity.

Why a Soulful Healer's Journey Demands Embodiment

Embodiment is essential for trauma healing because trauma can cause us to disconnect from or abandon parts of ourselves. However, our bodies are not merely receptors of experiences; they hold deep wisdom and are gateways to our wholeness. Our bodies express a spectrum of signals—from joy to discomfort to distress. Recognizing this, we should not only listen to our bodies when in discomfort or pain but also engage with them actively and consistently as a full embrace of life.

We live in our bodies, navigating countless feelings every moment. We often don't notice the many sensations our bodies feel, and this can make us feel disconnected. Embodiment is a foundational practice of presence, a proactive attunement to life's rhythms, bypassing the cognitive mind's chatter for a direct experience of being.

> *We live in a society that is left-brain dominant. Mental intelligence is valued over emotional, intuitive, and somatic intelligence. Empowering ourselves and others to access intelligence that emerges from the underused right brain is crucial to a balanced and healed way of living.*

For Soulful Healers, this is not merely about cognitive under-standing; it's about ensuring the teachings are vibrantly lived. This authenticity builds trust and deepens the therapeutic relationship. If we teach ourselves and our clients to honor our dynamic bodies and their wisdom, we ground ourselves in the present, infusing our routines with an embodiment as a sacred act.

Critical to these methods are the therapist's sensitivity and personal embodiment. Without acknowledging our own somatic experiences, we struggle to guide our clients. Through our embodi-ment, we adeptly navigate clients back to their body wisdom.

> *When you meet your client, grounded, centered, and attuned to your body's wisdom, it's not only words that come across but your vibration of living fully in your body that enables you to walk the talk.*

Our toolkit must be diverse and attuned, offering the proper somatic intervention resonating with the client.

Soulful Exercise: Meet the Library of Embodiment and Somatic Practices and Tools

In Chapter 5, we explored a selection of exercises, including somatic exercises for optimal vitality, to incorporate into your Vitality Planner. This included energy harmonization through self-Reiki, aligning the physical and energetic body with intentional movement and yoga practice, and fostering inner tranquility through meditation with intention. These practices lay the foundation for a vibrant and centered presence.

As we move deeper into the embodiment journey in this chapter, let's expand on that groundwork with additional somatic practices. These new tools are designed to enhance your connection to your body's wisdom and the whispers of your Soul further.

1. *Inquiries and Questions*

Integrate open-ended questions focused on embodiment into your sessions. Here are some examples to guide clients toward greater body awareness and Inner Wisdom:

What do you notice in your body?

What arises?

Where do you feel it in your body?

What sensations are alive in you right now?

Where does your breath flow freely, and where is it held?

If your body could speak, what would it say?

2. *Body Scan for Awareness*

Teach clients the practice of a body scan to cultivate a conscious awareness of their body as the home of the Soul:

- Begin at the feet, gradually moving attention up through each part of the body, listening to the body and the Soul.

- ↻ Encourage noticing areas of tension or relaxation without judgment.
- ↻ Invite reflection on how these sensations may correlate with emotional states.

3. *Listening to the Body*

- ↻ Guide clients in developing their listening skills to their body as an echo of the Soul.
- ↻ In Sessions:
  Teach your clients to listen to their bodies by bringing their awareness to their physical responses.
- ↻ For Practice at Home:
  Encourage clients to spend time each day tuning into their body's signals. This will help them learn how their body communicates, increasing their understanding of themselves.
- ↻ For Self-Regulation:
  Advocate its use during intense experiences to help clients manage and understand their reactions.

4. *Breath as a Somatic Compass*

Our breath loves to leave and enter our bodies, to leave and return. The pause between the exhalation and the inhalation allows us to connect. This natural, automatic process happens long before we become aware of the gift of intentional breathing.

Breathwork encompasses diverse techniques like diaphragmatic breathing, rhythmic breathing, and four-square breathing. Observe your client's patterns to tailor interventions that regulate their somatic and emotional states by paying close attention to how your clients breathe in different situations. This individualized approach ensures that the breathing practices are most effective for their unique needs and experiences. Encourage gentle exploration and practice techniques yourself first to guide with empathy and understanding.

I highly recommend that you learn from a breathwork professional as I did. This process has enriched my personal and professional life in ways that words cannot describe.

5. Grounding Techniques for Centering

Enhance grounding techniques by guiding clients to tune into their body's sensations. Invite them to visualize roots growing from their feet to cultivate a profound sense of stability and presence. Instruct them to notice the points where their body makes contact with solid surfaces—the feet firmly on the floor, the body supported by the seat, and hands resting on their thighs or touching another part of the body. Guide them to bring their attention to their breath, feeling the rise and fall of their belly, to help anchor them in the present moment and foster a sense of calm centeredness.

6. Intentional Movement

Intentional movement returns as a theme throughout the different chapters of this book. Despite previously covering it, I find it crucial to mention it again due to its profound impact. This practice is one of the strongest embodiment tools that has transformed my presence and practice.

Engaging in intentional movement involves moving with intention and awareness. This can be explored through various forms, such as yoga, tai chi, qigong, or even slow, mindful stretching. For me, a personal favorite is choreographing repeated movements to music that resonates with my Soul, using repetition as a moving mantra. This can then organically transition into free movement, allowing the music to guide the flow and expression of the body. Time and again, intentional movement has served as a pivotal moment for both me and my clients to overcome mental barriers, initiating or deepening the healing process.

Begin with small steps and discover a form of movement that resonates with you, one that you can engage with wholeheartedly and enjoy the freedom it brings.

7. Tension Release with Jacobson's Relaxation

Developed by American physician Edmund Jacobson in the early 20th century, Jacobson's Progressive Muscle Relaxation is a technique that helps identify and release tension. It involves tightening and then relaxing each muscle group, promoting an awareness of physical stress and the relief that follows. Practicing this method can enhance bodily control and deepen relaxation, offering a tangible experience of letting go, both physically and emotionally.

8. *Sensory Grounding: 5-4-3-2-1 Method*

Guide clients through the 5-4-3-2-1 technique to anchor them in the present. This practice typically involves:

- Naming five things you can see
- Acknowledging four things you can touch
- Listening to three things you can hear
- Identifying two things you can smell
- Noting one thing you can taste

9. *Self-Holding and Self-Hugging Techniques*

These two powerful techniques were created by Dr. Peter Levine, a renowned expert in trauma therapy and the creator of somatic experiencing, a body-focused approach to healing trauma and stress disorders. They are designed to tap into the autonomic nervous system and foster a sense of safety and calm.

The self-holding practice involves placing one hand on the forehead and the other on the back of the head, providing comfort, particularly when feeling overwhelmed or disconnected.

The self-hugging variation, where one hand rests under the armpit and the other on the opposite shoulder, offers a soothing embrace, mimicking the warmth and security of a hug.

By using gentle touch, these techniques aim to help release tension, reduce feelings of distress, and foster a deeper connection with one's bodily sensations. This can be particularly beneficial in the process of healing from trauma, because it encourages a reconnection with the body in a safe and controlled way.

10. *Butterfly Hug for Comfort and Self-Soothing*

The butterfly hug is a simple yet powerful technique to self-regulate and calm emotional turmoil, particularly in the face of trauma.

To practice this technique:

- ҂ Cross your arms over your chest, with your palms resting on your upper arms, just below the shoulders.
- ҂ Alternately tap your hands against your arms, like the gentle wings of a butterfly fluttering.
- ҂ Breathe deeply and evenly as you do this, focusing on the sensation and the rhythm.

This self-administered form of bilateral stimulation can help integrate emotional and cognitive processes, allowing for a sense of calm and collectedness. The rhythmic tapping mimics the bilateral stimulation used in EMDR therapy, helping to activate both hemispheres of the brain, which can contribute to processing and reducing the intensity of distressing memories or emotions. It is a compassionate gesture you can offer yourself any time you need comfort or reassurance.

11. *Connecting with the Body for Pain Recognition and Insight*

Pain is not just a physical sensation but also an intimate signal from the body, often reflecting deeper emotional states or neglected aspects of our well-being. *Encourage clients to foster a compassionate dialogue with their pain as a path to insight.*

This process involves several key steps:

- ҂ *Centering*: Begin with a few deep breaths to center oneself in the present moment.
- ҂ *Meditation*: Engage in a brief meditative practice to attune to the inner self, easing into a state of deep listening.
- ҂ *Conversing with Pain:* Direct the mind's focus to the area of discomfort and inquire with gentle curiosity, "What are you here to teach me?"

     ∿ *Listening*: Allow space for the body to respond. This could be in the form of a sensation, emotion, or even an intuitive thought or image.

     ∿ *Acknowledgment*: Whatever arises, acknowledge it without judgment.

     ∿ *Reflection*: Reflect in writing on the insights gained from this communication, considering how they might inform one's healing journey.

12. *Tapping: Emotional Freedom Technique (EFT)*

Tapping, introduced by Nick Ortner in "The Tapping Solution," merges ancient Chinese acupressure with modern psychology to address emotional issues. This method involves tapping specific meridian points while focusing on emotional distress.

Steps to Integrate Tapping:

    1. Identify the Issue: Concentrate on the emotional challenge.

    2. The Setup: Tap on the Karate Chop point, stating: "Even though I have this [problem], I deeply and completely accept myself."

    3. Tapping Sequence: Tap key points, initially verbalizing negative feelings to address the emotional disturbance, then shift to positive affirmations to promote healing:

       ∿ Eyebrow

       ∿ Side of the eye

       ∿ Under the eye

       ∿ Under the nose

       ∿ Chin

       ∿ Collarbone

       ∿ Under the arm

    4. Reevaluation: Assess and possibly repeat, adjusting focus based on changes in emotional intensity.

Tapping helps reduce stress, clear emotional blocks, and serves as a potent tool for emotional regulation, making it beneficial for both personal and therapeutic settings.

13. *Internal Family Systems (IFS) Approach: Self-Leadership and Parts Work*

The IFS model assists clients in identifying and healing wounded parts and cultivating the self's qualities, like confidence, openness, and compassion. This process acknowledges the coexistence of these varied inner aspects and their roles within the psyche.

Here's how to integrate IFS into somatic practices:

- ๗ *Identifying Parts:* Encourage clients to identify different "parts" of themselves, especially those activated in response to trauma or stress. These parts can often be felt somatically in the body, such as a tight chest when anxious or a heavy stomach when sad.
- ๗ *Building Relationships with Parts:* Guide clients to build an internal relationship with these parts, approaching them with curiosity, openness, and empathy, as they would in a dialogue with another person.
- ๗ *Accessing the Self:* Help clients to access their "Self," which in IFS is known as the seat of consciousness, and from this place, interact with the various parts. This Self-to-part connection can be felt as a somatic grounding and centering in the body.

A word about the last tool in the list: IFS.

As a committed advocate of holistic healing, I have consistently sought methodologies that respect our inner world's complex nature. Recognizing the risk of using healing and meditation as distractions from our genuine emotions, I have discovered profound significance in the IFS model. This therapeutic framework, which I have integrated into my professional practice, harmonizes with my dedication to genuine self-exploration and the healing process.

Developed by Richard C. Schwartz, IFS teaches us that within each of us resides a core Self, characterized by clarity, calmness, and connectedness, and that around this Self are various parts, often carrying burdens from past pain or trauma. By engaging with these parts directly, we can tune into our body and truly feel each emotion without falling into the trap of spiritual bypassing.

I wholeheartedly recommend exploring the IFS model to those leaning toward a holistic and empathetic healing path.

Let us return to the library of embodiment and somatic practices and exercises.

As you familiarize yourself with these practices, I encourage you to explore and learn each technique thoroughly before introducing them to your clients. Embodying and understanding these methods personally to facilitate them with confidence and sensitivity is essential.

Assess carefully for somatic readiness in your clients, and if you encounter fear or resistance it's wise to pause and take alternative paths. Somatic interventions can be revisited when a sense of safety and interest has been established, or it may be that, for some clients, these methods are not the appropriate choice. Your attunement to each client's unique journey is vital in using these powerful somatic practices ethically and effectively.

Maintaining the Window of Tolerance: Somatic Techniques in Trauma Healing

Before sharing a powerful story of trauma healing in a therapy session, it's essential to understand the concept of the "window of tolerance," a term coined by Dr. Daniel Siegel. This concept refers to the optimal zone of arousal where a person is able to function most effectively. When a person is within their window of tolerance, they can handle stress, process emotions, and remain connected with their present experience.

During trauma work, it's common for clients to swing between states of hyperarousal (overwhelmed, anxious, panicky) and hypoarousal (numb, disconnected, lethargic). The window-of-tolerance framework helps therapists recognize these states and guide clients back to a balanced state of arousal where healing can occur.

In the session I'm about to share, I used several somatic techniques from the collection presented in this chapter to maintain the client's window of tolerance. These practices were instrumental in supporting the client as we revisited their traumatic experiences.

Through an embodied approach to healing, we fostered a safe space where the client could explore their trauma with presence and awareness without stepping outside their window of tolerance. This is the delicate dance of trauma therapy: staying engaged with the difficult emotions and memories while remaining grounded in the body's wisdom.

> " *The somatic practices I employed served as anchors, gently holding the client in the here and now, allowing for the deep work of healing to unfold within the safety of their window of tolerance.* "

Soulful Snapshot

Ella, who was sexually abused in her childhood, had been seeing me for a few months, and she was now comfortable using body-focused exercises during our talks. We were ready to gently face a painful memory that had recently surfaced. To prepare, we chose some grounding techniques to help her stay present. We reviewed these techniques, like feeling her feet firmly on the ground and naming an object in the room that made her feel secure. She also practiced self-hugging, placing one hand under her armpit and the other on the opposite shoulder, and shared how it felt. I reminded her she could keep her eyes open or closed, whatever felt right for her.

As Ella used these techniques, I focused on creating a supportive energy around her. Being connected with life-force energy and with my Soul made me feel grounded, safe, and guided as I helped her. We then looked back on a memory of abuse from when she was 10. As she recounted her experience, I paid close attention to her body language and made sure she stayed within a comfortable emotional range.

Occasionally, I tuned into my internal guidance system for direction on how to proceed, ensuring I supported Ella in the best way possible.

When I noticed her becoming anxious, we paused for self-hugging, which helped her calm down. Then, using the IFS language, I guided her to talk to a wounded part of herself that was still hurt from those times. She conversed with this part, giving it kindness and understanding.

Soon, she was able to reach out to a more resourceful part of herself she named "The Voice." This part encouraged her to speak up and not see herself as a victim. Watching Ella take this step was moving. Over time, her anxiety decreased, and she became better at managing reminders of her past trauma on her own. She told me she could hear my encouraging voice in her mind, helping her regain her balance whenever needed.

As we shift from the deep exploration of trauma and embodiment, let us now turn inward, embarking on a journey through guided visualization to connect deeply with the wisdom of the body and the whispers of the Soul.

Guided Visualization: Grounding in the Now

Embodied mindfulness is the practice of fully living in the present moment with an awareness of the body's sensations, thoughts, and feelings. It is a grounding technique that invites us to witness the richness of our experiences without judgment and to open a pathway to the Soul. This deep presence allows us to access the Soul's wisdom, aligning our physical being with our spiritual essence.

When you are ready to begin the journey, find a comfortable position, take a deep breath, and listen to the audio you've downloaded, which is transcribed below.

> Let's journey into embodied mindfulness, uniting our physical sensations with our Soul's voice, grounding us in the here and now. Take a deep breath in, feeling the air fill your lungs, and

as you exhale, imagine releasing any tension or distraction. With each breath, become more present and aware of this moment.

Gently shift your attention to your body. Notice the points of contact where your feet meet the ground, and your body meets the chair. Feel the weight of your hands in your lap and acknowledge any sensations that arise. Turn your awareness to the top of your head. As you gently scan down, recognize each part of your body. Notice the forehead, eyes, jaw, and any sensations or wisdom each area holds.

Continue down to the neck and shoulders, arms, and hands. Observe any messages from the Soul as you move through your being. Flow your attention through your chest, back, and abdomen, feeling the energy of life and the Soul's light within. Proceed to your hips, legs, and feet. With each breath, feel more rooted, as if your feet are sinking into the earth, grounding you.

Find a spot within your body where you sense tension, heaviness, achiness, or fatigue. Allow yourself the time to gently find such a spot. When you've identified it, focus your attention there and become aware of your emotional response to this sensation. It's natural if you feel frustration or a desire for change regarding this discomfort. Whatever your reaction, acknowledge it with understanding. Approach these feelings with empathy, engaging in a compassionate inner conversation with this part of yourself. Affirm that it's acceptable for this sensation to exist and that you are present with it. Embrace the emotions that surface, offering them love and acceptance. Now, with kindness, invite your Soul into this dialogue.

Imagine a warm, gentle light within you, the light of your Soul. With each breath, let this light grow brighter, illuminating your inner world and bringing clarity to your mind and heart. Thank your Soul for loving you unconditionally, for her devotion to remain pure and be your essence. Allow your Soul to speak to you right now, in words, feelings, pictures, or an abstract knowing. Wait and listen.

Now, ask your Soul what she needs from you today. Listen for any messages or feelings that arise, embracing the Soul's guidance with openness and gratitude.

Contemplate on whether there is an action you can take to nourish your Soul, perhaps a small step or a meaningful ritual that would fulfill this inner need. Trust in the simplicity or depth of what comes forth, and if you choose to take action now—do it.

As you feel more connected to your body and Soul, affirm your presence in this space. Observe the environment around you, the air on your skin, the subtle sounds that usually go unnoticed. Imagine roots extending from your feet into the ground, connecting you to the earth's nurturing energy. Notice if you feel supported and stable, held by the present moment. Release any judgment or expectations and accept your feelings, whatever they are, with compassion.

Take a few more deep breaths, bringing this session to a close. When you're ready, gently open your eyes, returning to the room with a renewed sense of peace and a deeper connection to your body and soul.

Reflect on the Chapter: Questions to Consider

1. What new insights about the mind–body connection have you gained from this chapter?

2. How can the concept of the body as a "gateway to the Soul" be integrated into your daily mindfulness practices?

3. How can you incorporate the somatic tools discussed in the chapter into your professional work with clients?

4. What steps will you take to ensure you practice these somatic techniques ethically and effectively?

5. How can you continue to deepen your understanding and practice of somatic healing?

From Words to Action:
Applying This Chapter's Lessons

Transitioning from theory to practice is the essence of true learning, especially in the world of somatic healing and embodiment. The profound concepts in this chapter are not just to be read but to be lived. Embracing the body as a gateway to the Soul means honoring the complex dance between our physical sensations and our deeper emotional currents. It calls for attentive listening to the whispers of the body, acknowledging every signal as a message worthy of our respect and attention.

Not sure where to start? Begin with what brings a sense of curiosity in your body—maybe playing a song that touches your heart, closing your eyes, and moving freely. Or a simple yet profound practice of body scanning, not as a routine but as a sacred dialogue with your inner self. Let this be a time when you're not just scanning but also under-standing and integrating the Soul's narrative into your consciousness.

Tune into the wisdom of your Soul to discern which practices from this chapter resonate with your journey. Let this inner guidance inform the integration of these techniques into your personal and professional life.

Approach each client interaction with the awareness that their stories, like yours, are reflected in their somatic experiences. The grounding techniques, breathwork, and other somatic tools outlined here can be gentle guides that lead your clients toward stability and presence.

However, remember to do so with discernment and care as you integrate these practices. Assess readiness, obtain consent, and proceed only when you feel your client is safe and open to this profound work.

“ *With each step on this journey, recommit to being an embodied Soulful Healer who practices with authenticity, serves with empathy, and lives with intention.* ”

Unfolding the Next Layer

This chapter explored embodiment, embracing the body as a conduit to the Soul and the transformative power of integrating somatic practices into our personal and professional lives. This journey into the depths of our physical being reveals a path to profound healing, *a method to unlock the wisdom within our every cell, muscle, and breath.*

“ *We tap into a wellspring of resilience by cultivating a reliable sense of safety within our bodies. We learn that the body, often dismissed as an ordinary vessel, is a dynamic and intelligent entity capable of guiding us through the echoes of past traumas toward a future of well-being and wholeness.* ”

As we learn to listen to our bodies, we open the doors to our Soul, allowing its guidance to lead us in our practice and daily existence.

The benefits of such embodiment are many. It is the cornerstone of a Soulful Healer's practice, the silent strength behind our work. It brings richness to our professional lives and allows us to facilitate healing that is not only deep but also lasting.

By embracing these practices, we offer ourselves and our clients a blueprint for living rooted in authenticity and grounded in the present moment.

Integration: The Harmonious Fusion of the Six Keys

As we continue our journey to *becoming soulful,* we often find ourselves called to explore different dimensions of our lives and consider how well they align with our deepest values. This is a natural and enriching process, signaling growth and transformation. It might manifest as a reflective look at our dietary habits, the clothes we choose to wear, our hobbies, or the environments we cultivate around us.

I've witnessed individuals who, upon reconnecting with their souls, began to explore creative opportunities, write poetry, or even author books. Others have reignited long-held dreams, such as pursuing careers in acting or dancing. One of my clients, over 60 years old, embraced this journey and became a competitive dancer.

So, if you find yourself feeling an impulse to re-evaluate and possibly alter some areas of your life, welcome that change. It's an integral part of the expansion that complements the path of becoming more soulful. Embrace the changes and be open to the possibilities that your soulful journey is guiding you toward this evolution. Trust in the flow of transformation, knowing that each step brings you closer to a more authentic and aligned existence.

> *Becoming soulful means recognizing that every aspect of our lives—from the food we eat, to the clothes we wear, to the spaces we create around us, to the dreams we fulfill—presents a canvas to express our deepest values.*

Let's pause to recognize how each key—from Empowerment to Embodiment—uniquely contributes to *becoming soulful* in our personal and professional lives. These keys form the mosaic of our healing practices and create a holistic framework for soulful healing. They are not static concepts but dynamic practices that infuse our work with deeper meaning, guiding us to nurture healing spaces that resonate with the Soul's journey toward wellness and authenticity.

Empowerment, the first key, represents the core of our professional expertise and personal strength, aligning with our core values to expand our personal power.

Spirituality, the second key, blends our inner spirit with the larger forces of life. This mix helps balance our own energy with the wider world's, making us feel connected and whole.

Authenticity, the third key, fosters a deeper communion with our Soul, inviting the most genuine part of ourself to contribute to this symphony of growth.

Insight, the fourth key, infuses the process with Inner and Collective Wisdom, enriching the co-creation with layers of profound understanding.

The fifth key, *Vitality,* represents a deepened connection with life-force energy, infusing our actions with the force to move our life forward.

Finally, *Embodiment,* the sixth key, encourages us to wholeheartedly embrace our experiences and articulate our truths through our physical being, allowing our bodies to become vessels that carry and manifest our soul's intentions and our life's purpose.

Let the following illustration of the six keys be a map, your guiding star in your quest to elevate your healing presence in the world.

SIX KEYS FOR PROFOUND TRANSFORMATION

Empowerment
Reconnecting with personal & professional power

Spirituality
Developing a strong spiritual foundation

Embodiment
Embracing the body as a gateway to the soul

Soulful Healer

Vitality
Cultivating a bond with life-force energy

Authenticity
Nurturing a connection with the soul

Insight
Tapping into inner and collective wisdom

Soulful Snapshot: The Six Keys in Action

Early Struggles

As a child, Susan faced numerous challenges stemming from financial instability and a difficult home life. She grew up in a rented house that was considered old and weird by her peers, leading to feelings of discomfort and inadequacy. With her father's alcoholism contributing to a fear-based environment at home, Susan sought refuge in school, friends' houses, and books. Financial constraints were a constant, with the lack of money for school lunches or reliable phone service at home, and she often had to rely on welfare and navigate the associated stigma. Despite the hardships of frequently moving and living without basic utilities at times, Susan showed resilience by minimizing her own needs and comforting herself with the thought that others had it worse. Witnessing domestic abuse was another layer of her challenging environment, yet she found strength in her resolve to protect herself and her mother. Through all these difficulties, Susan held onto hope and the determination to create a better future for herself.

Healing Beginnings

Fast forward... After a commendable career as a police officer and enduring the loss of her ex-husband, who also struggled with alcoholism and was abusive, Susan found herself at a crossroads upon retirement. Feeling overwhelmed by a life of turmoil, she reached out to me. She used the word "chaos" when I asked her to describe her current life.

What began as a journey to find structure and order in life evolved into a profound healing process. As we worked together, we unpacked the deep-seated trauma from her childhood and marriage. Over the course of the year, Susan also went through my Reiki training, advancing to the level of Reiki Master. By building a consistent daily Reiki practice, she became engaged in the process of her self-healing. Using my holistic approach to trauma healing with Susan, which blends talk therapy with energy healing, spiritual practices, somatic techniques, and Soul work, led to a new level of happiness and satisfaction in life that she had not known before. She made significant strides in healing from her past trauma, cultivated a beautiful and peaceful home, and discovered joy in her relationships with others and, most importantly, with herself.

As Susan's journey of self-healing and personal growth progressed, she embraced further education, enrolling in various certification programs. She became an Eden Energy Medicine practitioner and obtained a ministering certification. These achievements, along with her mastery of Reiki, naturally guided her toward a path where she could make a significant impact on others.

Our private sessions evolved to focus on empowering Susan professionally as she transitioned into the next chapter of her life post-retirement. Reflecting on the process, it's fascinating to observe how the application of the six keys for elevating one's practice and presence facilitated Susan's development of a framework for helping others.

Soulful Evolution: Embracing the Six Keys to Professional Confidence

In the next phase of Susan's transformative journey, the first key, *Empowerment*, played a pivotal role. She tapped into her extensive professional expertise as an energy healing practitioner, Reiki Master, and trained minister, aligning these skills with her innate personal attributes. Crucially, Susan redefined her value system, choosing peace and joy as her guiding principles rather than the values inherited from her upbringing. This alignment extended to her personal values and those shared by the community of Soulful Healers she resonated with. A significant aspect of her empowerment was her ability to integrate the qualities and experiences from her police career, forging a cohesive identity as she embarked on crafting the next chapter of her life.

The second key, *Spirituality*, was instrumental for Susan to explore her spiritual beliefs—honed over the years and during her Reiki and ministry training—into a unique and strong spiritual foundation. This synthesis allowed her to infuse spirituality into her daily life in ways that were authentic and personally resonant. A meaningful turning point in her perspective happened in one session when we explored the consequences of her hesitation to be visible with her healing offerings.

The realization that others would continue to suffer if she did not step out in faith to offer her help (in her own words) gave her the courage to begin presenting herself as a professional.

The third key, *Authenticity*, was a transformative force in Susan's journey, bringing her into a deeper connection with her Soul. Her participation in an "Awaken your Intuition" course facilitated the blossoming of her intuitive abilities. Through practices like Soul Journaling and engaging in profound conversations with herself, she gained increasing clarity about her path. A momentous turning point occurred during her experience with the Journey into the Soul, a signature healing modality designed to facilitate direct guidance from the Soul, which led to profound healing and an elevated sense of clarity. This breakthrough allowed Susan to envision how she could integrate her various programs, courses, and certifications to forge an authentic and impactful presence in the world.

The fourth key, *Insight*, enhanced Susan's journey by incorporating a blend of personal insight and Collective Wisdom, offering her a new depth of clarity and direction. A pivotal moment for Susan was during an exercise with the Women of Wisdom cards (presented in Chapter 4), which are used as a tool to tap into one's Inner Wisdom. Remarkably, without prior knowledge of its image or message, Susan selected the card of Queen Sheba, who was known for her wisdom in biblical times.

In describing the card, Susan saw Queen Sheba as a courageous woman, unafraid to share her knowledge and stand confidently in her power, illustrated as having "open arms, open to receiving, a confident Queen," in Susan's words. The message and image on the card resonated deeply with Susan, aligning with a divine call to embrace her own wisdom and step forward to share it. This exercise also uncovered a childhood memory, revealing a nickname she was given, "queeny," which now took on new significance in the context of her current path. This connection between her past and her present journey illustrates the power of embracing one's Inner Wisdom and the signs that life presents, guiding her to a role where she could embody wisdom and empowerment.

The fifth key, *Vitality*, is the essence of life-force energy, essential for moving life forward. Susan's work with this key was interwoven with all aspects of our sessions, enriching both her personal healing journey and her professional development. She cultivated a strong Reiki practice, committing to self-treatment daily, which is a testament to the integration of healing the past while actively engaging in the present.

In a few months, Susan established a routine that included daily exercise and self-care practices, significantly enhancing her vitality. This balance of addressing past traumas while nurturing present well-being is a dual approach I uphold in my work with clients. Susan's dedication to this routine reflects her commitment to maintaining her vitality, which is a cornerstone for a life filled with energy and forward momentum.

The sixth key in Susan's transformative journey was *Embodiment,* which involves fully embracing her physical presence and integrating thoughts, emotions, and experiences into the body. During our sessions, I used various somatic techniques to guide Susan toward this key. Even though we were connected through Zoom, I remained attuned to her body's signals, such as changes in posture or facial expressions, and encouraged her to refocus on her physical sensations and reconnect with her body to reset.

I often invited Susan to ground herself and to explore how her thoughts and emotions resonated within her body. This practice helped her not only to intellectually understand her worth and unique gifts but also to feel and embody them viscerally. After working through the six keys, Susan's embodiment of her unique values as a professional healer became second nature. In one profound session, she articulated a statement that crystallized her self-recognition and values:

"I offer Lighthouse Healing Restoration Sessions. In my Spirit-led heart healing sessions, along with intuitive Reiki, sound healing, and energy medicine, I create a safe space for people to uncover their light, receive internal guidance, and gain an elevated perspective to restore balance and shine to their fullest capacity."

This statement evolved into her mantra, or "Passion Statement," and served as her guiding compass in her practice and personal growth.

I often encourage my clients to step back and look for the spiritual lessons that show up in their lives. Looking at Susan's life through the six keys of the Soulful Healer Method allowed her to become soulful and to see how each thread—challenges, losses, learnings, and awakenings—has been constructed into her being.

Her story is a beacon of hope, demonstrating that our past does not define us; instead, it sets the stage for a future we have the power to craft. Through her incredible commitment to personal growth and professional excellence, Susan has transformed her life from one of survival to one of thriving. Her journey, marked by the profound application of the six keys, stands as a testament to the possibility of rebirth at any stage of life.

I hope that Susan's journey reminds you that it is never too late to become the architects of your own destiny and that within you lies the natural power to become soulful and use the guidance you receive from within to elevate your presence and practice to extraordinary heights.

Where to Next:
You Can Change the World

Yes, you have that power! And no, perfection is not a qualification.

Healing is not reserved for the chosen few; it is a courageous journey we can all embark upon.

Growth and change do not occur in a straight line.

The process of personal growth looks more like a series of spirals, each one leading up to the next.

Consider this: No matter where you stand on this path, even when you find yourself in the depth of a spiral—at its lowest point—you are still further along than you were at the start of the previous one.

Our quest to become soulful mirrors this spiral progression. Ascending this spiral, we experience both peaks and valleys. It's important to periodically pause, look back at how far we have come on our spiral journey, and acknowledge our progress.

Can you envision your own spiral of growth among a sea of spirals, each belonging to other Soulful Healers?

Do you see how you are part of a collective of people, all dedicated to *becoming soulful*?

In our collective existence, the healing of one benefits the healing of all, forming a symbiotic relationship of restoration.

As we tend to our spirits, we cast ripples of healing across the world. You are more than just a traveler on this path to change—you are the path itself. Every step you take holds the power to change reality.

> *Each of us is a beacon—a solitary flame with the soulful power to pierce the darkest night. Alone, we are whispers of hope in the silence; together, we become a collective force that can transform the world.*

We have a world to change. And the change starts with us, guided by our Soul.

Remember: Regardless of what happens around you, she is always with you:

> She is the silent whisper of our inner truth,
> And a sacred flame that burns within.

> She embodies our core, the unaltered truth of who we are,
> A divine spark in the human form.

> Her needs are as deep as the ocean's heart,
> Craving emotions that rise and fall is vital as breath to our inner call.

> Yearning for love, unbound and wide,
> And compassion's embrace where true selves reside.

> In moments of silence and in life's loud art,
> At your core, she is there, apart.

> The untouched essence of your being so vast,
> Your most authentic self,

> Your Soul.

This collective power of transformation, *the symphony of Souls in healing*, is not distant from our personal stories. It is echoed in the silent companionship of my Soul, without whom this book would not exist. She has been an unwavering presence throughout my journey, from the weight of personal trauma to the realization of a healing spiral path that transcends my individual experience.

It is through acknowledging her whispers and the light she brings to the darkest corners of my being that I have been able to translate my path into a message, a brand, and a sacred mission to elevate consciousness, one Soul at a time.

In my darkest moments, my Soul infused me with light, and with each opportunity to show the way for someone else, my own path has grown brighter.

As we near the close of this journey, embracing the lessons and growth our Souls have experienced, it's my heartfelt belief that we each hold the power to craft our reality.

If a magical fairy granted me three wishes,

Wish 1 is for you:

A world where professionals rise in empowerment, standing tall and connected to their inner Soulful Healer. With access to the limitless wisdom held within their Souls, these practitioners ignite transformative healing insights. Guided and supported, they unleash their unique qualities, attributes, and gifts, making a remarkable difference by alleviating suffering and fostering profound global change.

Wish 2 is for those you serve:

In realizing my second wish, I envision those we serve—patients, clients, family, friends, and courageous souls—open and ready to embrace assistance. They feel empowered and guided, supported by professionals on their sacred healing journey and by the profound wisdom of their Souls. This inner guidance becomes a compass for them, steering their passage through the grand adventure of life.

Wish 3 is for us, a collective of Soulful Healers:

My final wish is to bring forth the Soulful Healer community, transcending the limitations of time and space to become a beacon of guidance and support. This community reaches across the globe, touching lives and fostering connections among countless individuals. In this sacred gathering, mutual respect and nurturing are the heart, cultivating an environment for openness and endless growth. Members shine as radiant beacons of healing, each embodying the six keys presented in this book: Empowerment, Spirituality, Authenticity, Insight, Vitality, and Embodiment. Together, this generation of Soulful Healers lives with integrity, uplifting one another and faithfully upholding the principles of the Soulful Healers Manifesto.

The Soulful Healers Manifesto

We stand together as a collective, knowing that healing together outshines healing alone.

We recognize the interconnectedness of the mind, body, spirit, and soul and champion an integrated approach to our sacred work.

We prioritize self-care.

We are humble yet confident in our gifts.

We navigate challenges with grace.

We listen to inner guidance, allowing our souls to speak.

We create safe spaces for healing.

We uncover root causes and lead with grounded wisdom.

As guides for transformation and self-discovery, we serve as conduits for healing, influencing the collective consciousness.

By embodying healing in our own lives, we facilitate healing in the lives of others.

Empowered to empower others, we create freedom inside and out.

Together, we infuse our lives with greater empowerment, spirituality, authenticity, insight, vitality, and embodiment.

In the symphony of healing, we are bound by a shared journey toward holistic well-being.

As one, we dance to the rhythm of our unique hearts and souls, expanding our impact and leaving a lasting mark on the world.

If there is nothing else I leave you with, let it be this: By journeying through this book, you have awakened the Soulful Healer within you.

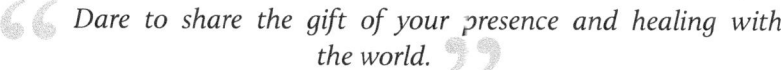

> *Dare to share the gift of your presence and healing with the world.*

As the final pages of this book unfold before you, we circle back to the manifesto that served as a beacon at the beginning of our journey together.

Its repetition here is not a mere echo of what has been but a reaffirmation of the promises and commitments we embraced at the start.

This manifesto, presented once again in these concluding moments, serves to reinforce the transformation within you that has been nurtured chapter by chapter. It is a deliberate pause, a moment to reflect on the distance traveled, and the growth attained.

As you stand on the threshold of what comes next, let this manifesto be both a familiar friend and a guiding star, reminding you of the essence of the Soulful Healer you have become. With this renewed pledge, may you step forward with clarity and courage, carrying the wisdom of these pages into the world that awaits your touch.

And now, as we embrace the manifesto's spirit in our daily lives, let us also commit to daily practices that embody this spirit.

A Daily Dose of Soul:
Infusing Soulfulness into Your Daily Life

At the beginning of your continued journey, I leave you with this invitation:

Infuse soulfulness into your daily life.

Create space each day to deeply connect with your source of wisdom: your Soul.

One dose of Soul per day is the essence of the art of becoming soulful. This moment is your Daily Dose of Soul, a vital ingredient on this transformative journey. Embrace it and let it guide you toward a life filled with purpose and presence. Every breath, every step, every heartbeat is an opportunity to live deeply, to bring forth the wisdom and beauty of your Soul. Start today, and let the soulful journey unfold.

Soulfully yours,

M. spiegl

Connect with Me
Visit our website to explore a wealth of supplementary
materials, like videos, audio tracks, and downloadable
worksheets that expand on the ideas discussed in this book.
Scan the QR code below for instant access.

https://beaconout.com/bsr
Let's keep the conversation going:
Email: info@beaconsofchange.com
Website: www.beaconsofchange.com

Soulful Gratitude

My heartfelt thanks go to everyone who has been a part of my journey, both personally and professionally. Your presence, support, and interaction have been invaluable. To those with whom I've faced challenges, I am equally thankful; you have been among my most significant teachers, offering lessons that have been crucial to my growth.

My Fellow Professionals

I extend my deepest gratitude to my fellow therapists, coaches, and healing professionals across the globe. Your dedication to healing, growth, and the well-being of others is the silent pulse that heals the heart of the world. Each session you conduct, each moment of insight you share, and each step you take toward nurturing the soulful journey of others echoes far beyond the walls of your practice. Thank you for embodying the spirit of a Soulful Healer and for the light you bring into the countless lives you touch.

Mentors and Teachers

I extend my sincere appreciation to all the mentors and teachers, both official and those serendipitously encountered along the way, who have enriched my professional development across the globe—from Israel to Germany, England to the United States. Your wisdom and guidance have not only polished my professional abilities but have also been instrumental in shaping my character. Thank you for making me a better professional and a more rounded individual.

Clients and Students

My gratitude extends to all my clients and students over the years who have pushed me to evolve and excel as a healer, teacher, mentor, and coach. Your challenges and questions have been the catalyst for my own growth. I extend a special thank you to those clients who have trusted me with their stories, allowing me to share them within these pages. Your trust has been a gift, and for that, I am truly thankful.

Pioneers of Practice

Many of the exercises, guided visualizations, and ideas in this book were refined through the dedication of a group of women in Atlanta. Anita Youngblood, Jackie Roginello, Julie Demenkow, Lauren Shelton, and Maria Gazzola formed the initial circle of Soulful Healers who tested my method. Your insightful feedback has been instrumental in shaping this book, and your encouragement was the wind beneath my wings throughout this writing journey. You began as strangers but completed this journey as true soul sisters, embodying the transformative power of the Soulful Healers' path.

Beacons of Change

To my dedicated team members, Dawn Goforth-Kelly and Rachel Craig, my heartfelt thanks for your unconditional love and support. Your patience and understanding, even when I felt lost or overwhelmed, have been nothing short of extraordinary. Thank you for holding the vision of this book's highest potential.

To my incredible community of women who joined me on this important mission to live, love, and lead at full power, thank you for being the beacons of change you were born to be and for sharing your light with the world.

Architects of the Written Word

Heartfelt thanks go to Kelly Irving, the best developmental editor I could have hoped for. You dismantled my first draft, and your keen feedback not only improved this book but also developed the book beyond what it was before your invaluable input. To my copy editor, Lu Sexton, your support and insightful inquiries have greatly improved the manuscript. Thank you for treating my creation with so much respect. Shawn Nook—thank you for the beautiful illustrations. And last but not least, Kam Bains, my extraordinary cover designer— your professionalism is unmatched, and your creative spirit deeply connected with the message of my book. With an artist's intuition and a professional's precision, you found a way to mirror my soul in your design, doing so with ease and affection that took my breath away.

First Impressions Circle

To four extraordinary women: Liz Fisch, Madeleine Goforth (who has also been my valued copywriter for many years), Laura Silverman, and Cindy Wander—the first to read the entire manuscript. You were trusted with being straightforward, and I am profoundly grateful for your honesty. Your feedback was the surge of inspiration I needed, enabling me to rewrite, expand, trim, and polish the prose until it sparkled with clarity and purpose.

Circle of Support and Vision

To all my friends and family members in Israel and the United States, thank you for believing in me and cheering me on along this journey. A special gratitude goes to the creator of the Women of Wisdom Oracle cards, my soul-sister Judith Jungman-Saadon, who was the first to have a clear vision of this book. Your ability to see the potential of this book before it was fully formed has been a source of strength and inspiration.

My Family

To Shmuel, my husband and partner in every sense—life, business, and now this book. Your presence and natural sense of balance allowed me to shut the world out and write. With champion skills and a remarkably bright mind, you've navigated the self-publishing world with finesse, transforming challenges into triumphs and elevating this book to its greatest potential. You've been my rock and anchor when things got too much, always ready with innovative ideas and ways to fix any problem. Your knowledge and expertise have been nothing short of instrumental in bringing these pages to life. And through every low and every high, your love is the constant force that carries me—thank you for ALWAYS being there.

Nadav and Noy, you two know the real me in all my colors, and you truly get me! Your honest feedback on the many little pieces of this big puzzle—writing and publishing a book—and the gentle way you understand my dreams and hopes have meant everything. Being your mom has filled, fills, and will always fill my Soul. Watching you grow, create, and carve out your own paths in life is my daily inspiration and my main source of joy.

NOTES

Chapter 1

Van der Kolk, B. (2015). *The body keeps the score: Brain, mind, and body in the healing of trauma.* Penguin Books.

Chapter 3

Moore, T. (2016). *Care of the soul, twenty-fifth anniversary ed: A guide for cultivating depth and sacredness in everyday life.* Harper Perennial.

Chapter 4

Jung, C. G. (1989). *Memories, dreams, reflections.* Vintage.

Doidge, N. (2007). *The brain that changes itself: Stories of personal triumph from the frontiers of brain science.* Penguin Life.

Doidge, N. (2016). *The brain's way of healing: Remarkable discoveries and recoveries from the frontiers of neuroplasticity.* Penguin Life.

Damasio, A. (2000). *The feeling of what happens: Body and emotion in the making of consciousness.* Mariner Books.

Hoffman Institute. *The Hoffman Quadrinity Process*® https://www.hoffmaninstitute.org

Ortner, N. (2013). The tapping solution: A revolutionary system for stress-free living. Hay House.

Jungman-Saadon, J. *The Women of Wisdom cards.* https://www.women-of-wisdom.com

Detrick, R. (2023). *Rewriting Eve: Rescuing women's stories from the Bible and reclaiming them as our own.* She Writes Press.

Chapter 5

McTaggart, L. (2008). *The field: The quest for the secret force of the universe.* Harper Perennial.

Singer, M.A. (2013). *The untethered soul: The journey beyond yourself.* New Harbinger Publications.

Brown, B. (2021). *Atlas of the heart: Mapping meaningful connection and the language of human experience.* Random House.

Shapiro, F., & Forrest, M. S. (2016). *EMDR: The breakthrough therapy for overcoming anxiety, stress, and trauma.* Basic Books.

Chapter 6

Van der Kolk, B. (2015). *The body keeps the score: Brain, mind, and body in the healing of trauma.* Penguin Books.

Centers for Disease Control and Prevention. (2021). The CDC-Kaiser Permanente Adverse Childhood Experiences (ACE) study. https://www.cdc.gov/violenceprevention/aces/about.html

American Psychiatric Association. (2022). *Diagnostic and statistical manual of mental disorders: DSM-5-TR* (5th ed., text rev.). American Psychiatric Association Publishing.

Levine, P. A. (2010). *In an unspoken voice: How the body releases trauma and restores goodness.* North Atlantic Books.

National Institute for the Clinical Application of Behavioral Medicine. (2013, April 3). *Trauma therapy webinar series: Interview with Peter Levine.* [Webinar].

Shapiro, F., & Forrest, M. S. (2016). *EMDR: The breakthrough therapy for overcoming anxiety, stress, and trauma.* Basic Books.

Ortner, N. (2013). The tapping solution: A revolutionary system for stress-free living. Hay House.

IFS Institute. *Internal Family Systems.* https://ifs-institute.com/

Schwartz, R. (2021). *No bad parts: Healing trauma and restoring wholeness with the Internal Family Systems model.* Sounds True.

Siegel, D. J. (2012). *Pocket guide to interpersonal neurobiology: An integrative handbook of the mind.* W. W. Norton & Company.

Ascending Vibrations. (2022). *Somatic trauma healing: The at-home DIY crash course in experiencing true body awareness through somatic secrets anyone can do & insider techniques your therapist doesn't want you to know about.* Ascending Vibrations.

About Michal Spiegelman

Michal Spiegelman is the visionary behind Beacons of Change, a transformative platform dedicated to guiding women and healing professionals toward a soul-fueled life, lived at full power. As the founder and creator of the Soulful Healer Method for Profound Transformation, Michal empowers a diverse community of individuals to find their authentic voice and develop a distinctive identity.

Michal combines deep expertise and timeless wisdom with a comprehensive methodology enriched by a variety of traditional and holistic therapeutic tools. This powerful blend ignites transformation and growth, inspiring women and healing professionals alike to become soulful and shine brightly as beacons in their personal and professional lives.

Many therapists, coaches, and healing professionals possess skills in established protocols, but Michal guides these dedicated practitioners beyond conventional training. By blending their seasoned expertise with the Soulful Healer Method's six transformative keys, they expand their therapeutic practice with integrity, purpose, and soul.

Michal holds degrees in social work and music education. As a medical intuitive, certified professional life coach, Reiki Master, and spiritual mentor, she is passionate about raising consciousness in the world, one soul at a time.

Michal's work is characterized by a holistic, trauma-informed approach that empowers people to awaken to the wisdom of their Souls—to become soulful.

When she's not working or writing, music and art give her a daily dose of soulfulness. She loves to paint, play the piano, dance, and cook healthy food, which nurtures her body and soul. Michal starts and ends her day with self-Reiki, meditation, and intentional movement with music.

Michal and her husband were born and grew up in Israel and have lived in Germany and the US. They reside in Atlanta, Georgia, and have two young adult children who are creating their own paths in life.

Visit Michal's website at www.beaconsofchange.com

About The Soulful Healer Programs

Become a Soulful Healer: Join one of the Soulful Healer Training Programs.

Our Professional Advancement programs provide professionals, such as therapists, coaches, and healing practitioners, with tools to deepen and enrich their practice and create an identity that sets them apart from others in their field.

Our Personal Transformation programs offer guidance to individuals on their self-discovery journey, enhancing their ability to become more soulful and make lasting, positive impact in their own lives and those around them.

www.beaconsofchange.com/soulful-healer

If You Loved Becoming Soulful

I poured my heart and Soul into the pages. If *Becoming Soulful* moved you, please help us spread the message.

- Review *Becoming Soulful* on Amazon and Goodreads.
- Post a recommendation on social media, in your newsletters or blog, tagging @michalspiegelman #BecomingSoulful #SoulfulHealer
- Recommend me as a guest for podcasts, TV and radio shows, newsletters, blogs, or other social media platforms.

It takes a tribe. You are my tribe. Thank you!

www.ingramcontent.com/pod-product-compliance
Lightning Source LLC
Chambersburg PA
CBHW060518130626
46553CB00002B/551